OPERATION
TOTALIZE 1944

The Allied drive south from Caen

STEPHEN A HART

ILLUSTRATED BY JOHNNY SHUMATE
Series editor Marcus Cowper

First published in Great Britain in 2016 by Osprey Publishing,
PO Box 883, Oxford, OX1 9PL, UK
1385 Broadway, 5th Floor, New York, NY 10018, USA
E-mail: info@ospreypublishing.com

A CIP catalogue record for this book is available from the British Library.

ISBN: 978 1 4728 1288 9
PDF e-book ISBN: 978 1 47281289 6
e-Pub ISBN: 978 1 47281384 8

Editorial by Ilios Publishing Ltd, Oxford, UK (www.iliospublishing.com)
Index by Alan Rutter
Typeset in Myriad Pro and Sabon
Maps by Bounford.com
3D bird's-eye views by The Black Spot
Battlescene illustrations by Johnny Shumate
Originated by PDQ Media, Bungay, UK
Printed in China through Worldprint Ltd.

16 17 18 19 20 10 9 8 7 6 5 4 3 2 1

THE WOODLAND TRUST

Osprey Publishing are supporting the Woodland Trust, the UK's leading
woodland conservation charity, by funding the dedication of trees.

LIST OF ACRONYMS AND ABBREVIATIONS

AFV	Armoured fighting vehicle
AP	armour-piercing
APC	Armoured personnel carrier
AOK	Armeeoberkommando (Army Command)
AVRE	Armoured Vehicle Royal Engineers
HE	high explosive
HEAT	high-explosive anti-tank
LMG	light machine gun
LSSAH	1.SS-Panzer-Division Leibstandarte SS Adolf Hitler
OBW	Oberbefehlshaber West (Supreme Command West)
OKW	Oberkommando der Wehrmacht (Armed Forces High Command)
OP	observation post
PIAT	Projector, Infantry, Anti Tank
RAC	Royal Armoured Corps
SMG	submachine gun
SPG	self-propelled artillery gun
TCV	troop-carrying vehicle
USAAF	United States Army Air Force

Key to military symbols

CONTENTS

The strategic situation in Normandy, 1–8 August 1944.

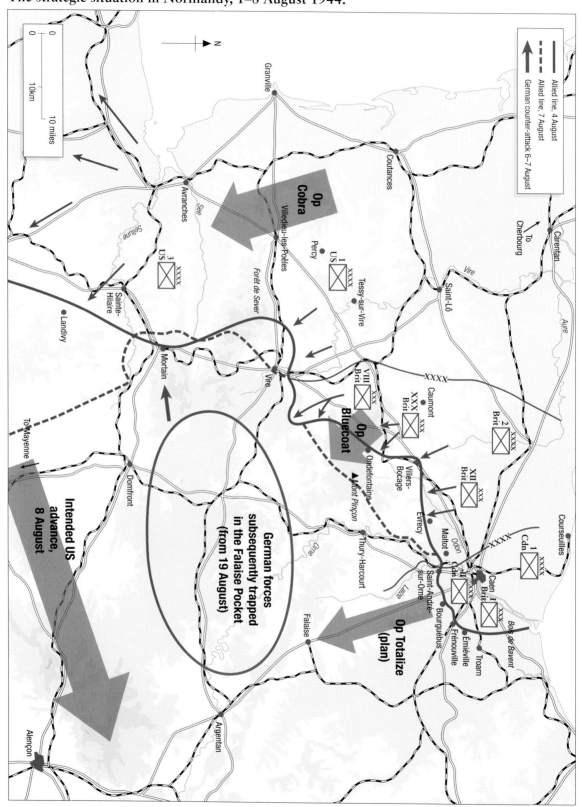

ORIGINS OF THE CAMPAIGN

After the successful 6 June 1944 Allied D-Day landings on the coast of German-occupied Normandy, the Anglo-Canadian 21st Army Group only managed to fight its way slowly inland in the face of bitter German resistance. Following the demise of its strategy of immediately repelling the invasion, the German Oberbefehlshaber West (OBW – Supreme Command West) ambitiously attempted during June to throw the invaders back into the sea with armoured counter-attacks. When this unrealistic strategy failed, Hitler insisted that OBW's forces mount an unyielding defence from their current positions. This aimed to deny the Allies the space required within the bridgehead for the assembly of follow-on forces, the dumping of supplies and the creation of airfields. While this strategy slowed the Allied advance inland, it also locked the German forces into a bitter attritional struggle against powerful Allied forces backed by massed supporting fires from artillery, naval guns, tactical airpower and heavy aerial bombers.

Next, on 18 July the British Second Army's VIII Corps launched Operation Goodwood, an attempt to outflank Caen from the east. Notwithstanding the heavy losses incurred, Goodwood (and its Canadian flank operation, Atlantic) did capture the remainder of Caen. This success moved the Allied front forward onto the Bourguébus Ridge, which overlooked the open country south towards Falaise. Subsequently, further west on 25 July the US First Army launched Operation Cobra and by the 27th had achieved a decisive breakthrough which it ruthlessly exploited to cross the Sélune River at Pontaubault on 31 July. By reaching the Cotentin peninsula's south-western corner the American forces opened up the possibility of rapid advances west into Brittany, south towards the Loire and east towards the Seine: US First Army and the newly operational US Third Army audaciously exploited these opportunities with rapid advances in all directions. Meanwhile, the British Second Army shifted its forces westwards, launching Operation Bluecoat around Caumont on 30 July to prevent German armour moving west to block the deluge of advancing American armour. Meanwhile Lieutenant-General Guy Simonds' II Canadian Corps continued to hold the Bourguébus Ridge along the British Second Army's eastern flank. On 23 July, however, Simonds' corps came under command of Lieutenant-General Henry Crerar's newly operational First Canadian Army. Subsequently, II Canadian Corps mounted Operation Spring during 25–26 July to secure limited gains on the ridge; the operation was largely unsuccessful and incurred heavy casualties.

On 28 July the 21st Army Group commander, General Bernard Montgomery, discussed future operations with Simonds. Montgomery wanted II Canadian Corps to mount a major offensive from the Bourguébus Ridge to tie down German armour, thus preventing the latter being sent west to stem Bluecoat or the American advance. The realisation of this intent became Operation Totalize – the set-piece II Canadian Corps offensive that struck south-south-east to capture the high ground north of Falaise which dominated the lateral road passing through the town. Between 28 July and the operation's initiation on 7 August, however, the strategic situation was transformed. First, at Hitler's behest, during 6–7 August the Germans mounted an armoured counter-offensive from Mortain towards Avranches to cut off the American forces that had already surged south. It not only failed but also pushed the German 7.Armee west, creating an emergent Allied double envelopment; for the Americans were already surging east from Mortain towards Alençon to create the southern shoulder of this envelopment.

By 7 August, therefore, Allied domination of the lateral road through Falaise took on renewed significance: it would block German retreat west out of the forming pocket and serve as a springboard for Simonds' forces to strike south to link up with the American units in the Argentan–Falaise area, thus sealing the pocket of encircled enemy forces. Simonds, meanwhile, had reached two conclusions in the wake of his corps' abortive 25–26 July Spring offensive: first, the terrain in this key German 'hinge' sector favoured the defenders, so any offensive would meet formidable resistance, probably spearheaded by elite Waffen-SS formations; second, his two Canadian divisional commanders had displayed command inadequacies, and thus the forthcoming operation would need to be carefully planned at corps level and then 'gripped' during its execution if it was to succeed.

CHRONOLOGY

1944

30 July	II Canadian Corps Commander Lieutenant-General Guy Simonds is ordered to begin planning an offensive towards Falaise launched from the Bourguébus Ridge, slated to commence in ten days time.
1 August	Simonds' 'Appreciation of Situation' outlines five prescient observations from which he draws a tactical deduction concerning how the offensive must be executed. These deductions form the basis for Totalize.
3–6 August	British and Canadian personnel hastily convert 76 surplus M7 Priest fully tracked self-propelled guns into armoured personnel carriers (APCs) in the ad-hoc Workshop 'Kangaroo' to provide the troop lift capacity required for the seven mobile columns that will spearhead Totalize Phase I.
5 August	The original II Canadian Corps plan is issued.
5–6 August	The 1.SS-Panzer-Division Leibstandarte SS Adolf Hitler (LSSAH) withdraws from its defensive positions facing II Canadian Corps, being replaced by the arriving 89.Infanterie-Division. The Oberkommando der Wehrmacht (OKW – Armed Forces High Command) had dispatched the LSSAH westward towards the American breakout sector, but Simonds' intelligence staff believed that the division had withdrawn to bolster the German reserve defence position along the sector that opposed the II Canadian Corps.
6 August	After intelligence is gained about these changes to the enemy's dispositions, Simonds issues the revised II Canadian Corps plan.
7 August, 2200–2300hrs	As darkness falls, the Totalize assault forces – seven mobile columns and five infantry battalions – move forward to their forming-up positions along the II Canadian Corps' start line.
7 August, 2300–2340hrs	An initial heavy bomber strike on five targets located on the flanks of the imminent Totalize ground assault is mounted by 642 RAF Bomber Command heavy night bombers.
7 August, 2330hrs	Start of the initial break-in operation (Totalize Phase I) spearheaded by seven mobile columns, which advance behind a rolling barrage delivered by 360 artillery pieces.
8 August, 0205–0340hrs	Two of the Canadian mobile columns reach the designated debus area at Pièce-de-Caillouet, having advanced almost 6km deep into enemy lines.
8 August, 0700hrs	Five of the seven Allied mobile columns have by now secured or closed in on their objectives, including Hill 122. The advance of the remaining two columns, however, has been halted short of their objectives by fierce German resistance.
8 August, 0800–1230hrs	The Phase I assault forces consolidate their gains in the Caillouet–Hill 122–Saint-Aignan-de-Cramesnil area.

8 August, 1230–1355hrs Second (daylight) bombing strike against the second German defensive position (which runs from Bretteville-sur-Laize through to Saint-Sylvain) mounted by United States Army Air Force (USAAF) Boeing B-17 Flying Fortresses.

8 August, 1220–1340hrs German counter-attack north towards Gaumesnil and Saint-Aignan-de-Cramesnil mounted by elements of Kampfgruppe Waldmüller consisting of four Tiger tanks, ten tank destroyers, 20 Panzer IVs and Vs, plus around 550 Panzergrenadiers.

8 August, *c*.1250hrs During the hasty German local counter-attack towards Saint-Aignan-de-Cramesnil, SS panzer ace Michael Wittmann is killed when his Tiger tank explodes after being hit by Allied fire.

8 August, 1355hrs Start of Totalize Phase II. The Polish 1st and 4th Canadian Armoured divisions strike south against the German reserve defence position after the US heavy bombing strikes have ended.

8 August, 1800hrs The Canadian infantry of Les Fusiliers Mont-Royal, backed by British Crocodile flame-throwing tanks, finally overwhelm the dogged German resistance in the bypassed forward defended locality of May-sur-Orne, on the offensive's western flank.

8 August, 2100hrs Angry at the lack of forward momentum achieved on the afternoon of 8 August, Simonds orders an improvised continuation of the advance through the night to be executed by two infiltrating armoured battle groups.

9 August, 0400hrs An improvised all-arms task-force, Worthington Force Battle Group (WFBG), commences its advance south from near Gaumesnil. Its mission is to mount an audacious 7.6km advance south-south-west to seize the key high ground of Hill 195 north of Fontaine-le-Pin.

9 August, 0630hrs After a confused night advance, WFBG reaches and secures what it believes to be its objective, Hill 195; in fact it has inadvertently seized high ground on the Hill 140 ridge feature, some 6.5km east-north-east of its objective.

9 August, 2100hrs After facing repeated SS counter-attacks throughout the day, the surviving remnants of the lost and isolated WFBG are finally overrun.

10 August, 2000hrs 8th Canadian Infantry Brigade, from 3rd Canadian Infantry Division, backed by elements from 2nd Canadian Armoured Brigade, assault the German positions in Quesnay Wood in order to rekindle forward momentum in the stalled Totalize offensive. Fierce German resistance soon stymies the new Allied assault.

11 August, 0330hrs Recognising that Totalize has stalled irrevocably, Simonds orders the termination of the offensive. In the previous 76 hours, Simonds' forces have secured an advance up to 16.2km deep into the German lines across a frontage up to 14.2km wide. Nevertheless, Totalize has still failed to achieve its final objectives, capturing the high ground north of Falaise.

OPPOSING COMMANDERS

The Allied planning and execution of Totalize, as well as the German resistance to it, owed much to the plans, decisions and personalities of the respective senior commanders involved in the battle. The following section provides brief pen pictures of the key Allied and German commanders who took part, as well as that of one infamous SS junior officer.

ALLIED COMMANDERS

Lieutenant-General Henry Crerar (commander, First Canadian Army) was born in Ontario in 1888. He served as a gunner lieutenant-colonel during World War I before serving as Director of Military Operations in 1935. During World War II he served as a divisional and corps commander before in early 1944 assuming command of First Canadian Army, which was earmarked for the Normandy campaign. During the 1944–45 North-West Europe campaign Crerar had a strained relationship with his superior Montgomery, due to two interconnected issues: Crerar's dogged insistence on upholding Canadian national interests, and Montgomery's low opinion of Crerar's command capabilities. The coalition dynamics involved prevented Montgomery from employing Canadian formations with the same latitude as British ones. The two senior officers had already clashed during the 1942 Dieppe Raid, during which Crerar threatened to refer the dispute to the Canadian government, thus forcing Montgomery to back down. While a keen advocate of full co-operation with the British, Crerar refused to surrender Canadian national interests for the greater good or operational convenience of the 21st Army Group. Crerar, for example, was reluctant to allow Canadian formations to serve outside Canadian higher command. Montgomery's modest opinion of Crerar's abilities was based on a dislike of Crerar's reliance on his staff for his ideas, his involvement in wider Canadian military issues and his reluctance to work from verbal orders.

Seen on the left, Lieutenant-General Henry Crerar participates in a planning briefing for Totalize on 4 August together with Montgomery (centre, in pullover) and between them Air Marshal Sir Arthur 'Mary' Coningham. (Library and Archives Canada PA-129122)

Lieutenant-General Guy Simonds (commander, II Canadian Corps) was born in England in 1903. He was commissioned from the Royal Military College of Canada at Kingston with the Sword of Honour in 1925 into the Canadian Horse Artillery. During the 1930s he passed the British Staff Course at Camberley and was an instructor at the Royal Military College of Canada at Kingston. Starting World War II as a mere major, he undertook several command and staff appointments as part of his meteoric rise to assume command of II Canadian Corps in January 1944. After the war his career reached its zenith when he was appointed Chief of the Canadian General Staff in 1951. Simonds is today considered by some historians as one of the most effective Anglo-Canadian corps commanders of the 1944–45 North-West Europe campaign. He brought focus, self-confidence and firm direction to the conduct of his corps' operations, as well as an inclination to adopt novel methods (as manifested in Totalize Phase I). However, others have criticised him for his neat engineer's mind that produced highly complex plans and his limited understanding of armoured formations (as evidenced by the narrow frontages given to his two armoured divisions during Totalize Phase II). From a British perspective, the Anglophile Simonds was a more flexible coalition commander than Crerar, since he was willing to subordinate Canadian national interests to the needs of Allied operational convenience.

Major-General Charles Foulkes (commander, 2nd Canadian Infantry Division) played a key role in Totalize, spearheading the initial night infiltration break-in assault in the sector west of the main Caen–Falaise road. Foulkes was a dour commander who excelled at internal bureaucratic politics. Born in England in 1903, Foulkes joined the Canadian Militia in 1922. Four years later he transferred to the Canadian Permanent Force, into the Royal Canadian Regiment. After passing the British Staff Course, Foulkes served overseas during 1939 with the 1st Canadian Infantry Division. Subsequently he commanded the 2nd Canadian Infantry Division during the Normandy campaign. Prior to Totalize the 2nd Canadian Infantry Division achieved some success in Operation Atlantic (the Canadian element to the British Operation Goodwood), but suffered heavy casualties in the process. In November 1944 Foulkes assumed command of I Canadian Corps in Italy before becoming Chief of the Canadian General Staff from 1945 to 1951.

Major-General Rodney Keller (commander, 3rd Canadian Infantry Division) had over his military career earned a reputation for being a tough 'soldier's soldier'; however, by early August 1944 the demands of command had begun to take its toll on him. Born 1900 in England, 'Rod' Keller graduated from the Royal Military College of Canada at Kingston in 1920 and was commissioned into the Princess Patricia's Canadian Light Infantry. Keller left Canada as a brigade-major with the 1st Canadian Infantry Division in 1939 and took command of the 3rd Canadian Infantry Division in September 1942. Keller's handling of his division during its 4 July 1944 assault on Carpiquet village and airfield caused his British superiors to doubt his fitness for command. Consequently, generals Montgomery, Dempsey and Crocker passed

Major-General Rodney Keller, the commander of the 3rd Canadian Infantry Division in July 1944. (Library and Archives Canada PA- 116519)

On the left Major-General Rodney Keller welcomes his fellow divisional commander, Major-General Charles Foulkes, in a posed official photograph sometime in July 1944. (Library and Archives Canada PA-129134)

recommendations to Crerar that Keller be sacked. Keller was a favourite of Crerar, however, who believed he could be a potential corps commander. Thus the First Canadian Army commander handed judgement over to Keller's new superior, Simonds. When Simonds confronted Keller with these adverse reports, Keller asked to be medically boarded. However, with no obvious competent alternative officer to replace him with, both Simonds and Crerar decided not to relieve him of his command at this juncture. During the second heavy bombing strike in Totalize Keller was unfortunately wounded by friendly fire and evacuated out of theatre.

The II Canadian Corps commander Lieutenant-General Guy Simonds (right) and 4th Canadian Armoured Division commander Major-General George Kitching (left) seen in England prior to D-Day. (Library and Archives Canada PA-132650)

Major-General George Kitching (commander, 4th Canadian Armoured Division) was born in 1910 in China. Kitching commissioned into the British Army's Gloucestershire Regiment after undertaking military training at the Royal Military College Sandhurst. After resigning in 1938, he joined the Canadian Army with the Royal Canadian Regiment. During 1940–43 he served in a number of command and staff appointments. Next, in October 1943, after promotion to the rank of brigadier, he commanded 11th Canadian Infantry Brigade (part of the 5th Canadian Armoured Division). Promoted major-general in March 1944 he then assumed command of the 4th Canadian Armoured Division, which he led during the battle of

Normandy. Sacked by Simonds in late August 1944, Kitching later served as Brigadier, General Staff in I Canadian Corps from November 1944 through to July 1945. He served in various senior appointments during his lengthy post-war career (1945–65).

Major-General Stanisław Maczek (commander, Polish 1st Armoured Division) was born in 1892 near Lwów in modern-day Poland. Maczek was conscripted into the Austro-Hungarian Army during World War I and served in a mountain unit on the Dolomites front. He joined the newly formed Polish Army after the end of the war and soon developed an interest in mobile operations. During the autumn 1939 Axis invasion of Poland Colonel Maczek commanded the Polish 10th Armoured Cavalry Brigade. Maczek's command fought a number of successful withdrawal actions before its personnel were interned in neutral Hungary. Maczek and most of his troops then moved to France where the 10th Brigade was reformed with French equipment. Maczek's brigade fought effectively during the May–June German invasion of France, before being extracted to the United Kingdom. This unit formed the nucleus of what became the Polish 1st Armoured Division, equipped with British and American-supplied vehicles. On 1 August 1944 Maczek's division arrived in Normandy and was allocated to Simonds' corps. In 1947 Lieutenant-General Maczek was demobilised by the Allies and had his Polish citizenship stripped by the new communist Polish government. Disgracefully denied a British war service pension, he worked as a barman in Edinburgh, Scotland. Not until 1990 did the post-communist Polish regime reinstate his general's rank and pension. He died in Scotland in 1994 aged 102.

Allied war correspondents talk with Major-General Stanisław Maczek (right), the commander of the Polish 1st Armoured Division, at Amblie, France, 7 August 1944. (Library and Archives Canada PA-129140)

GERMAN COMMANDERS

General der Panzertruppe Heinrich 'Hans' Eberbach (commander of 5. Panzerarmee) was born in Stuttgart in 1895. He served in World War I both on the Western Front and in the Middle East and rose to the rank of lieutenant. During the interwar years he served in the police and then rejoined the German Army in 1935. He commanded armoured units during the 1939 Polish and 1940 Western campaigns before leading an armoured brigade during Operation Barbarossa, the summer 1941 Axis invasion of the Soviet Union. He took command of 4.Panzer-Division in April 1942. Next, on 3 July 1944 with the rank of General der Panzertruppe he assumed leadership of the German strategic reserve in the West, Panzergruppe West, then locked into bitter defensive battles in Normandy; this command was soon thereafter renamed 5.Panzerarmee. On 9 August 1944 5.Panzerarmee was split into two, with one part (named Panzergruppe Eberbach) staying under his control, and the rest (still designated 5.Panzerarmee) being taken over by Josef Dietrich, the former commander of I SS-Panzerkorps. Having fortunately managed to escape from the Falaise pocket during mid-August, Eberbach was captured by advancing British forces on 31 August.

    SS-Oberstgruppenführer Josef Dietrich (commander, I SS-Panzerkorps) was born in Bavaria in 1892. Dietrich rose from the rank of private in 1911 to become by 1944 one of the highest ranking Waffen-SS officers of the entire war, and one of just two such officers to command an army in the field. Dietrich joined the Nazi Party and the SS in 1928. Thereafter, due to his intimate contact with Hitler he soon rose through the SS hierarchy to command the Leibstandarte, Hitler's bodyguard unit; in 1934 Dietrich directly participated in the bloodletting of the night of the long knives. He continued to command the Leibstandarte as it was successively enlarged to become a division by 1940, and thereafter through until July 1943 when he took command of the newly raised I SS-Panzerkorps. By this time he had been promoted to SS-Oberstgruppenführer (colonel-general), only the second Waffen-SS commander ever to obtain this rank. On 9 August 1944, in the midst of the Totalize offensive, the OKW promoted Dietrich to command 5.Panzerarmee after its former commander, Hans Eberbach, took control of the ad-hoc Panzergruppe Eberbach. Subsequently, Dietrich commanded 6.Panzerarmee, which fought first in the December 1944 Ardennes counter-offensive and then during spring 1945 in Hungary and Austria. Back on 6 August 1944, the day before Totalize commenced, Dietrich became just the 16th recipient of the coveted Knight's Cross with

The commander of 5. Panzerarmee, General der Panzertruppe Hans Eberbach, talks to a Canadian interpreter after being captured by British forces on 31 August 1944. (Library and Archives Canada PA-189586)

Oak Leaves, Swords and Diamonds, an extremely rare, high honour only ever awarded to just 27 individuals.

SS-Brigadeführer Kurt Meyer (commander, 12.SS-Panzer-Division 'Hitlerjugend') was born in December 1910 to working class parents. From 1929 Meyer worked for the Mecklenburg police. In 1930 he joined the Nazi Party and the SS the next year as an other rank. After commissioning in 1932 he quickly rose through the ranks of the SS officer corps, and served with the Leibstandarte in the 1939 Poland and 1940 Western campaigns as a company commander. During the 1941 Axis invasion of the Soviet Union Meyer earned himself a formidable reputation as the audacious commander of the reconnaissance regiment of the Leibstandarte. During 1943 the now SS-Standartenführer (colonel) Meyer took command of SS-Panzergrenadier-Regiment 25 in the newly raising 12.SS-Panzer-Division 'Hitlerjugend', the slated sister formation to the Leibstandarte. Meyer spurred his regiment to fanatical resistance during the early days of the Normandy campaign. On 14 June 1944 division commander SS-Brigadeführer Fritz Witt was killed by Allied naval gunfire and Meyer took command of the 'Hitlerjugend' division. On 1 August he was promoted SS-Oberführer (senior colonel) and led the division's attempts to halt the Totalize offensive during 7–10 August. On 6 September, the newly promoted SS-Brigadeführer (brigadier) Meyer was captured by Allied forces. In 1946 he was sentenced to death, later commuted to life imprisonment, for his complicity in the numerous war crimes 'Hitlerjugend' personnel inflicted upon Allied prisoners during the early days of the Normandy campaign.

SS-Hauptsturmführer Michael Wittmann (commander, 2.Kompanie, schwere SS-Panzer-Abteilung 101) was, by the time of his death on 8 August 1944, one of Nazi Germany's leading Tiger tank aces. Born in April 1914, he saw service with the elite Leibstandarte during the 1939 Polish campaign and commanded an assault gun platoon during the 1941 conflict in the Balkans. During 1941–43 Wittmann served in the war against the Soviet Union, where he soon racked up a significant number of enemy tank kills, for which he received the Iron Cross First Class and promotion to SS-Oberscharführer (sergeant). After officer training SS-Untersturmführer (second lieutenant) Wittmann rejoined the Leibstandarte in December 1942. While serving with the division's Tiger-equipped 13.schwere Kompanie Wittmann again performed well during the July 1943 battle of Kursk, thanks to his careful planning of actions and the unshakable composure he maintained during combat. From late 1943 Wittmann served as a Tiger tank commander in schwere SS-Panzer-Abteilung 101. In early 1944 Wittmann was promoted to SS-Obersturmführer (lieutenant) and received the coveted award of the Oak Leaves to the Knight's Cross for his tally of 92 enemy kills. On 13 June 1944 Wittmann's 2.Kompanie of schwere SS-Panzer-Abteilung 101 inflicted a costly repulse on the British 7th Armoured Division at Villers-Bocage; for the cost of four Tigers, Wittmann's command destroyed 12 British tanks and 24 other armoured vehicles. Finally, in the early afternoon of 8 August 1944 Wittmann – now an SS-Hauptsturmführer (captain) – was killed during a hastily enacted counter-attack launched in the vicinity of Saint-Aignan-de-Cramesnil.

OPPOSING FORCES

The execution of the Totalize offensive, and the ensuing development of the individual actions within it, owed much to both sides' respective force structures, weapons, equipment, doctrines, tactics and techniques. This chapter provides a brief overview of these critical aspects that helped determine the unfolding of the offensive.

ALLIED

The Allied forces that undertook Totalize came under the command of Simonds' II Canadian Corps. This corps headquarters became operational in Normandy on 9 July and soon took command of all the Canadian formations then in Normandy, namely the 2nd and 3rd Canadian Infantry divisions, together with the 2nd Canadian Armoured Brigade. At this point the corps remained subordinated to Lieutenant-General Miles Dempsey's British Second Army. On 23 July, however, Lieutenant-General Henry Crerar's First Canadian Army became operational, taking command of Simonds' corps alongside Lieutenant-General John Crocker's British I Corps. Both corps were then deployed on the eastern flank of the Normandy bridgehead. By the time that Simonds' corps had initiated Totalize, his headquarters controlled five divisions and two independent brigades (an atypically large number): the 2nd and 3rd Canadian Infantry divisions, the British 51st (Highland) Infantry Division, the Polish 1st and 4th Canadian Armoured divisions, together with the British 33rd and 2nd Canadian Armoured brigades. Other supporting forces under Simonds' command included specialised armour from the British 79th Armoured Division and four Army Groups, Royal Artillery or Royal Canadian Artillery. In total, Simonds' forces included 91,000 front-line troops, 720 artillery pieces and 930 armoured fighting vehicles (AFVs), in addition to enjoying the support of 3,150 Allied aircraft.

Three crewmen from the Highland Light Infantry struggle to manoeuvre a 6pdr anti-tank gun across the baked dry ground on 6 August 1944. (Library and Archives Canada PA-131365)

While II Canadian Corps' forces included units from three nationalities – British, Canadian and Polish – these forces invariably deployed the same weapons and equipment, as well as having almost identical force structures and tactical doctrines. They thus represented interchangeable elements of a seamless British Commonwealth/European exile military machine. During Totalize Simonds' forces employed four main groups of weapons against the Germans: direct fire weapons (tanks and other AFVs), as well as anti-tank guns and launchers); indirect fire support assets (artillery, heavy mortars and rocket launchers); aerial fire support (tactical aircraft and heavy bombers); and platoon-level small arms (rifles, machine guns and trench mortars).

The principal AFVs employed by Simonds' forces were the M4 Sherman and M4 Sherman Vc Firefly medium tanks, and the A27 Cromwell cruiser tank; four models of specialised AFVs were also employed. In terms of other anti-armour assets, the Allied forces also deployed the 6pdr and 17pdr anti-tank guns, as well as the PIAT infantry anti-tank launcher. The M4 Sherman was the standard tank deployed in the three armoured regiments each fielded by the 2nd Canadian Armoured Brigade, and the Polish 1st and 4th Canadian Armoured divisions, as well as each armoured division's armoured reconnaissance regiment. Within each troop of four Sherman tanks in these armoured regiments, however, one tank was the up-gunned variant, the Sherman Firefly. The M4 Shermans fielded by Simonds' forces were either the M4A2 (Sherman III) or the M4A4 (Sherman V) variants. The Sherman V weighed 30 tons, possessed armour protection up to 3.2in. thick, and mounted the M3-MV 75mm gun. By the 1944 Normandy campaign the Sherman's standard of survivability was decidedly modest while its lethality was equally unimpressive at normal combat ranges of around 1,000m against the heavier German tanks – the Panzer V Panther and the Panzer VI Tiger.

Instead of the M3-MV 75mm gun, the Sherman Firefly sported the potent 17pdr gun in a slightly modified chassis. The Firefly Vc weighed 37.7 tons and its gun could destroy any German AFV at 1,000m (a reality seldom raised in discussions of Allied tank inferiority). In lethality the Firefly actually outperformed the German Tiger and matched that of the King Tiger, although this potential lethality was hampered by the tank's modest survivability (exacerbated both by its distinctive long-barrelled silhouette and the obvious flash on firing). In addition, the armoured reconnaissance regiment of the Polish 1st Armoured Division was equipped with A27 Cromwell cruiser tanks rather than the 75mm-gunned Sherman, with one Sherman Firefly per troop of four vehicles. The Cromwell weighed 27.6 tons, possessed armour protection up to 3in. thick, and mounted a 75mm gun; its general performance was broadly equivalent to that of the Sherman.

A column of Sherman tanks from the Polish 1st Armoured Division kick up dust as they move along a dusty road in Caen towards a bridge over the Orne River, during the morning of 8 August 1944. (Library and Archives Canada PA-128955)

In addition to these tanks Simonds' forces also deployed several units of specialist armour from the British 79th Armoured Division. To clear the mines laid as part of the German defensive line, several troops of Sherman Crab flail mine-clearing tanks from the British 1st Lothians and Border Yeomanry took part in the mobile column assault. The Crab was simply a standard Sherman tank (with its main armament retained) fitted with twin jibs to the front that held a rotating chain device that detonated enemy mines. The second specialised AFV employed by Simonds' forces was the Churchill Armoured Vehicle Royal Engineers (AVRE) assault vehicle. This was a modified Churchill Mark III tank with a fixed turret in which was mounted an 11.4in. Petard spigot mortar that fired a 28lb warhead designed to destroy enemy concrete bunkers. Simonds' forces also employed the fearsome Churchill Crocodile flame-throwing tanks of the British 141st Regiment, Royal Armoured Corps (RAC).

The crew of a Sherman Firefly pose for the cameraman by sitting astride the long barrel of the tank's potent 17pdr gun in the days prior to Totalize. (Library and Archives Canada PA-138413)

In terms of indirect fire support assets to assist the assaulting infantry and armour, II Canadian Corps deployed 720 artillery pieces. By this stage of the war Allied artillery was highly effective, being able to bring large

A column of Crusader Mark II/III anti-aircraft tanks, equipped with twin 20mm guns, from the Polish 1st Armoured Division move forward to cross the Orne River in Caen, during the morning of 8 August 1944 prior to initiating Phase II of the offensive. (Library and Archives Canada PA-116249)

Canadian 5.5in. artillery guns lay down a barrage, while in the foreground vehicle-mounted infantry move forward. (Library and Archives Canada PA-130167)

amounts of accurate fire quickly onto a designated spot as required. Simonds' indirect fire assets consisted of 384 field guns (that is, 25pdr and 105mm field guns), 288 medium and heavy guns (of between 5.5in. and 7.2in. calibres), and 48 heavy anti-aircraft guns. The field guns had 600 rounds per gun forward dumped, and the other pieces 300 rounds per gun. These capabilities enabled the Allies to deliver indirect fires on a much larger scale (total number of rounds delivered) at greater intensities (total rounds fired per minute) for a much longer duration than could their German counterparts.

The standard Anglo-Canadian field piece, the British Ordnance QF 25pdr gun, weighed 1.6 tons and was crewed by a team of six; its 3.4in. gun could fire up to eight 25lb high explosive (HE) rounds per minute over a distance of up to 12,200m. The heaviest gun, the BL 7.2in. howitzer, weighed 9.8 tons and was crewed by a team of ten; its gun could fire up to three 202lb HE rounds per minute over a distance of 15,400m. In addition, II Canadian Corps' assaulting forces also enjoyed considerable aerial support from either tactical air assets or heavy strategic bombers. The tactical aircraft employed included the Supermarine Spitfire Mk IX, the de Havilland Mosquito and the Hawker Typhoon. Three types of heavy

Lorries tow British artillery guns forward along the main Caen–Falaise road between Vaucelles and Lorguichon during Phase II of Totalize. (Library and Archives Canada PA-138493)

bombers were employed to support Totalize – RAF Bomber Command Halifaxes and Lancasters plus USAAF B-17 Flying Fortresses – which delivered bomb payloads of between 8,000 and 14,000lb.

At the micro-tactical level Totalize revolved around the close combat actions of infantrymen. Often operating alongside direct-fire assets such as tanks and backed by indirect artillery fire, platoons of Allied assault infantry endeavoured to advance through the hail of enemy defensive fire. The latter were delivered by a similar mix of German small-arms rounds, direct-fire assets such as AFVs and the indirect fire support of artillery and heavy mortars. At full strength, each of Simonds' rifle infantry platoons deployed 37 troops organised into a platoon headquarters and three 10-man sections. Each platoon fielded three Bren light machine guns (LMGs), 29 Lee-Enfield Mk IV rifles, two Sten guns, one 2in. mortar, and a PIAT anti-tank launcher.

The Bren LMG was the main sectional weapon, with the rifle fire of the rest of the section often serving to protect the fire effect of the Bren. Firing magazines of 26 rounds, the Bren could deliver fire of between 60 and 450rpm out to an effective range of 730m. While a reliable and accurate weapon, the Bren's sustained rate of fire compared unfavourably with that of the equivalent German section LMG, the MG42. The combination of the tactical fire superiority of the MG42, with the fact that the Germans were typically on the defensive, often made it difficult for Allied assault infantry to advance successfully to close to contact with the defending Germans.

The Lee-Enfield Mk IV single-shot bolt-action rifle was the main II Canadian Corps platoon small arm, with eight men in each section equipped with this weapon, plus five personnel in platoon headquarters. Weighing 9lb and using five-round charger clips, the Mk IV delivered 0.303in. rounds out to a normal combat range of 600m. The platoon commander and three section commanders and platoon lead mortar operator each carried the Sten submachine gun (SMG). Weighing 7lb the 9mm Sten delivered 500rpm of suppressive fire out to an effective range of 73m. The sole platoon indirect fire weapon was the 2in. mortar; this fired a 2.5lb high-explosive or smoke round out to a maximum range of 430m. Each platoon also normally fielded one attached direct-fire anti-tank weapon – the PIAT launcher. This fired a HEAT (high-explosive anti-tank) round and could penetrate most enemy armoured vehicles at close ranges of under 100m.

An officer from the Highland Light Infantry has a much-needed hair wash, courtesy of the assistance of a captain colleague, during the final preparations for Totalize on 6 August 1944. (Library and Archives Canada PA-114506)

GERMAN

Just like the attacking Allies, the Germans defending the Bourguébus Ridge also deployed a similar mixture of weapons, including direct fire anti-tank assets, indirect fire weapons, and small arms; in contrast with the Allies, however, the defenders enjoyed only extremely limited tactical air support. The German direct fire anti-tank assets included tanks, tank destroyers, anti-tank guns and personal infantry launchers. The main tanks fielded by the 12.SS-Panzer-Division 'Hitlerjugend' were the Panzer IV Ausf. H or J (deployed in I Bataillon of the division's armoured regiment) and the Panzer V Ausf. G Panther tank (in this regiment's II Bataillon). Entering service during March 1943, the 24.6-ton Panzer IV Ausf. H mounted a 48-calibres long 7.5cm gun and possessed armour protection up to 3.2in. thick; the Ausf. J manifested similar characteristics. In terms of technical performance (the mix of lethality, survivability and mobility), the Panzer IV was broadly comparable to the standard M4 Sherman, and the Germans lost large numbers of these tanks during the bitter struggle for Normandy. The Ausf. G Panther weighed 44.1 tons, mounted a 70-calibres long 7.5cm gun and possessed well-sloped armour protection of up to 3.2in. thickness. The Panther outperformed Allied tanks in terms of combined lethality and survivability. In addition to these two tank types, the division's SS-Panzerjäger-Abteilung 12 also deployed Jagdpanzer IV tank destroyers. This vehicle weighed 23.7 tons and mounted the Panzer IV's 7.5cm gun fitted in a low-silhouetted fixed superstructure. On 7 August, the elements of the much-depleted 'Hitlerjugend' division located in the Totalize battle space fielded 20 Panzer IVs and Panthers, and 12 Jagdpanzer IVs.

In addition to these divisional AFVs, I SS-Panzerkorps also deployed the dozen operational Panzer VI Ausf. E Tiger I heavy tanks then fielded by schwere SS-Panzer-Abteilung 101, a corps troops unit. Operated by a five-man crew, this squat, angular leviathan weighed 55.1 tons. Despite this bulk the tank could obtain a reasonable maximum road speed of 24mph but its cross-country mobility was poor. The Tiger possessed formidable lethality – its powerful 56 calibres-long 8.8cm KwK 43 gun could penetrate the frontal armour of most Allied tanks at combat ranges of up to 1,800m. The Tiger possessed heavy levels of protection that made it invulnerable to standard 75mm-gunned Sherman fire at normal combat ranges of 750–1,000m. During Totalize, I SS-Panzerkorps tactically grouped these Tigers with the tanks of the 'Hitlerjugend'. In terms of combined lethality and survivability the Tiger I outperformed all Allied AFVs, only being matched in lethality by the less survivable Sherman Firefly.

A frontal view of a German Panther tank showing its well-sloped armour; 12. SS-Panzer-Division 'Hitlerjugend' deployed ten of these effective tanks during Totalize, alongside a similar number of operational PzKpfw IVs. (Library and Archives Canada PA-114984)

In terms of other anti-tank assets I SS-Panzerkorps deployed two anti-tank gun models and the Panzerfaust, a shoulder-launched infantry weapon. I SS-Panzerkorps' most numerous anti-tank gun was the 7.5cm PaK 40, the standard weapon in an infantry division's anti-tank battalion. The 89. Infanterie-Division fielded 12 such guns alongside 12 8.8cm flak guns being used in the anti-tank role. Firing armour-piercing (AP) rounds the PaK 40 could penetrate 5.2in. of vertical armour at 460m. A much rarer, yet even more potent, anti-tank gun was the 8.8cm PaK 43 which utilised the same gun as the King Tiger. Only available in small numbers, this weapon served in just two independent army-level units, the Artillerie-PaK-Abteilungen 1039 and 1053. A few of these units' 8.8cm PaK 43 guns buttressed I SS-Panzerkorps' defence of the Bourguébus Ridge. Finally, the German infantry deployed an effective short-range personal anti-tank weapon, the Panzerfaust. This one-shot weapon consisted of a disposable launcher tube that fired a HEAT shaped-charge warhead. The main tactical disadvantage is that troops employing the Panzerfaust often had to get within 35m of enemy armour to achieve a kill.

In addition to these direct fire weapons, I SS-Panzerkorps' forces fielded a range of indirect fire weapons, including artillery and rocket launchers. The 89.Infanterie-Division (like most such formations) fielded two types of artillery guns: the 10.5cm leFH 18 light field howitzer and the 15cm sFH 18 heavy field howitzer. The 10.5cm gun weighed 1.95 tons and fired a 33lb shell out to a maximum range of 10,675m. The 15cm howitzer weighed 5.4 tons and could fire its rounds out to an effective maximum range of 13,260m. Typically, both of these guns were horse-drawn weapons, although some pieces might be towed by a half-tracked carrier. German armoured divisions such as the 'Hitlerjugend' instead deployed the self-propelled artillery gun (SPG) variants of these weapons, the 10.5cm Wespe (Wasp) and the 15cm Hummel (Bumblebee) vehicles. Based on the Panzer II chassis, the 10.8-ton Wasp carried 40 rounds for its 10.5cm leFH 18/2 gun. The heavier Hummel, which utilised the composite Panzer III/IV chassis, carried 18 rounds for its 15cm sFH 18/1 howitzer. Both vehicles' guns delivered an identical performance to the horse-drawn variants discussed above.

Personnel from the Canadian Film and Photo Unit inspect a captured German 88mm anti-aircraft gun near Bayeux, France, during August 1944. This weapon proved highly effective in the anti-tank role during Totalize. (Library and Archives Canada PA-131349)

By mid-1944, however, the German artillery arm was in a sorry state and compared very unfavourably with the highly effective Allied artillery. German artillery units suffered from a paucity of good quality personnel, equipment shortages, limited mobility, and a chronic dearth of munitions, as well as enduring the privations imposed by complete Allied aerial superiority and effective Allied artillery counter-battery fire. To augment their relative lack of effective indirect fire support, therefore, the Germans in Normandy employed mobile Nebelwerfer rocket launchers. The 15cm Nebelwerfer 41 (NbW 41) wheeled launcher fired a salvo of six spin-stabilised rockets out to a maximum range of 6,900m with a rate of fire of three salvoes in five minutes. To avoid destruction by Allied air power the Germans employed their rocket launchers in 'shoot and scoot' tactics; the Germans prepared multiple firing positions for their launchers and as soon as they fired the weapon they would move it to another location before Allied sound ranging located it and a tactical air strike or artillery counter-battery fire ensued. Through such tactics the survivability of Nebelwerfer launchers remained high. In addition to the corps-level SS-Werfer-Abteilung 101, with 24 launchers when at full strength, the 'Hitlerjugend' also deployed SS-Werfer-Abteilung 12 (with four batteries each of six 15cm launchers) and attached elements of Werfer-Regiment 83.

In addition to these direct and indirect fire weapons, the numerous infantry platoons deployed by I SS-Panzerkorps also fielded a range of small arms. The MG42 machine gun was the main German sectional heavy weapon, with (as with the British) the rifle fire of the rest of the section serving to protect the fire effect of this weapon. The MG42 was the finest machine gun of World War II. Thanks to its quick-change barrel arrangement and superb engineering, the MG42 could achieve sustained rates of fire much greater than that of the Bren. Its fire also produced an unmistakable staccato 'brrrppp' sound that had a noticeable psychological effect on Allied troops.

An NCO identified as Company Sergeant-Major Vassie uses a wooden box containing grenade priming materials on the eve of Totalize, 7 August 1944. (Library and Archives Canada PA-132912)

The remainder of the German infantry section wielded the 7.92mm Karabiner (Kar) 98b carbine rifle. Weighing 9lb, this single-shot bolt-action rifle was operated using a five-round clip and had an effective range of up to 460m.

In order to wield these weapons and equipment effectively to resist Totalize, the German forces needed to be organised into an appropriate force structure. In early August 1944 SS-Oberstgruppenführer Josef Dietrich's I SS-Panzerkorps, an elite higher command created back in July 1943, defended the Bourguébus Ridge. By spring 1944 I SS-Panzerkorps controlled the elite 1. and 12.SS-Panzer divisions; consequently, it was often committed to wherever a particularly significant battle was unfolding. Given this elite status, the corps' subordinate forces tended to be well equipped and possessed above average personnel strengths. The corps also fielded an above average range of corps troops units (all numbered 101) which included a signals, heavy tank, artillery, mortar, rocket-launcher and flak battalion.

The I SS-Panzerkorps subordinate formation that bore the brunt of Totalize Phase I was Generalleutnant Konrad Heinrichs' 89.Infanterie-Division. Raised in February 1944 and worked up in Norway, the division had a reduced front-line rifle strength of six grenadier battalions plus a fusilier battalion (a dual purpose reconnaissance and reserve unit). With a high proportion of young soldiers, the division had close to the normal establishment of heavy weapons; it was also a horse-drawn formation with limited tactical mobility. In addition, the 12.SS-Panzer-Division 'Hitlerjugend' together with schwere SS-Panzer-Abteilung 101 played a key part, alongside the battered 89.Infanterie-Division, in the German defence against Totalize Phase II.

The 'Hitlerjugend' division commenced forming during March 1943 as part of the German total war mobilisation undertaken after the debacle at Stalingrad. Mobilised from 16- and 17-year-old volunteers from the heavily Nazified Hitler Youth movement, most of the division's officers and senior NCOs were drafted in from the infamous LSSAH. By spring 1944 the division deployed 150 AFVs and 20,500 personnel, but remained chronically short of junior NCOs. After almost completing its training programme by D-Day, the OKW immediately committed the division to fighting in Normandy.

During the bitter battles fought during that summer the indoctrinated personnel of the 'Hitlerjugend' demonstrated both an impressive offensive spirit and a fanatical defensive resilience; sadly what went alongside these traits was the perpetration of heinous war crimes. During the period 7–12 June 'Hitlerjugend' personnel murdered at least 155 unarmed Allied prisoners in 35 separate incidents. This fanatical defensive determination was seen several times during Totalize, for example during Sperrgruppe (Blocking Group) Klein's defence of Haut Mesnil. During Totalize the division's headquarters was in the Château Le Mont Joly, just to the east of Potigny. Adjacent to this HQ were two observation posts established on rocky outcrops on either side of the Laison Gorge at La Brèche au Diable and the *Tombeau de Marie Joly*, well-chosen locations that would impact on the unfolding of Totalize.

Two other German infantry divisions played a minor role in resisting Totalize. On the eastern flank, elements of the 272.Infanterie-Division held the front east of Garcelles-Secqueville on the extreme left flank of Simonds' advance. Similarly the 271.Infanterie-Division, subordinated to the adjacent corps, held the line west of the Orne River and thence south through Laize-la-Ville; some of its units became involved in actions on the extreme western flank of the Allied advance. In addition to these four divisions, I SS-Panzerkorps also deployed a range of corps troops, including two independent motorised artillery battalions. Finally, the Luftwaffe-controlled III Flakkorps deployed a number of 2cm, 3.7cm and 8.8cm anti-aircraft guns in the area south of the Bourguébus Ridge, some of which became involved in the defence against Totalize.

The 12.SS-Panzer-Division 'Hitlerjugend' established a carefully located observation post on top of the *Tombeau de Marie Joly* shrine, located on the eastern side of the Laison Gorge east of Potigny. The divisional headquarters was located close by at the Château Le Mont Joly. (Author's collection)

ORDER OF BATTLE

ALLIED FORCES

II CANADIAN CORPS (7–10 AUGUST 1944)

Polish 1st Armoured Division

Polish 10th Armoured Cavalry Brigade
- Polish 1st Armoured Regiment
- Polish 2nd Armoured Regiment
- Polish 24th Lancers Regiment
- Polish 10th Dragoons Regiment

Polish 3rd Infantry Brigade
- Polish 1st Highland Rifle Battalion
- Polish 8th Rifle Battalion
- Polish 9th Rifle Battalion

Divisional units
- Polish 10th Mounted Rifle Regiment (armoured recce)
- Polish 1st Anti-tank Regiment
- Polish 1st Motorised Field Regiment
- Polish 2nd Motorised Field Regiment
- Polish 1st Light Anti-aircraft Regiment

2nd Canadian Infantry Division

4th Canadian Infantry Brigade
- Royal Regiment of Canada
- Royal Hamilton Light Infantry
- Essex Scottish Regiment

5th Canadian Infantry Brigade
- Black Watch of Canada
- Régiment de Maisonneuve
- Calgary Highlanders

6th Canadian Infantry Brigade
- Les Fusiliers Mont-Royal
- Queen's Own Cameron Highlanders of Canada
- South Saskatchewan Regiment

Divisional units
- 8th Reconnaissance Regiment (14th Canadian Hussars)
- 2nd Canadian Anti-tank Regiment
- 4th Field Regiment, Royal Canadian Artillery
- 5th Field Regiment, Royal Canadian Artillery
- 6th Field Regiment, Royal Canadian Artillery

3rd Canadian Infantry Division

7th Canadian Infantry Brigade
- Royal Winnipeg Rifles
- Royal Regina Rifles
- 1st Canadian Scottish

8th Canadian Infantry Brigade
- Queen's Own Rifles of Canada
- Régiment de Chaudière
- North Shore Regiment

9th Canadian Infantry Brigade
- Highland Light Infantry of Canada
- Stormont, Dundas and Glengarry Highlanders
- North Nova Scotia Highlanders

Divisional units
- 7th Reconnaissance Regiment
- 3rd Canadian Anti-tank Regiment
- 12th Field Regiment, Royal Canadian Artillery
- 13th Field Regiment, Royal Canadian Artillery
- 14th Field Regiment, Royal Canadian Artillery

4th Canadian Armoured Division

4th Canadian Armoured Brigade
- Governor General's Foot Guards (21st Armoured Regiment)
- Canadian Grenadier Guards (22nd Armoured Regiment)
- British Columbia Regiment (28th Armoured Regiment)
- Lake Superior Regiment

10th Canadian Infantry Brigade
- Algonquin Regiment
- 1st Battalion, Argyll and Sutherland Highlanders (Princess Louise's)
- Lincoln and Welland Regiment

Divisional units
- South Alberta Regiment (29th Armoured Reconnaissance Regiment)
- 5th Canadian Anti-tank Regiment
- 15th Field Regiment, Royal Canadian Artillery
- 23rd Field Regiment, Royal Canadian Artillery

51st (Highland) Infantry Division

152nd Infantry Brigade
- 2nd Seaforth Highlanders
- 5th Seaforth Highlanders
- 5th Queen's Own Cameron Highlanders

153rd Infantry Brigade
- 5th Black Watch
- 1st Gordon Highlanders
- 5th/7th Gordon Highlanders

154th Infantry Brigade
- 1st Black Watch
- 7th Black Watch
- 7th Argyll and Sutherland Highlanders

Divisional units
- 2nd Derby Yeomanry (reconnaissance)
- 1st/7th Middlesex (machine gun)
- 6th Anti-tank Regiment
- 126th Field Regiment, Royal Artillery
- 127th Field Regiment, Royal Artillery
- 128th Field Regiment, Royal Artillery

2nd Canadian Armoured Brigade

1st Hussars (6th Canadian Armoured Regiment)

Fort Garry Horse (10th Canadian Armoured Regiment)

Sherbrooke Fusiliers (27th Canadian Armoured Regiment)

33rd Armoured Brigade

144th Regiment, Royal Armoured Corps

148th Regiment, Royal Armoured Corps

1st Northamptonshire Yeomanry

Corps troops

Elements 79th Armoured Division

141st Regiment, Royal Armoured Corps (Crocodiles)

1st Border and Lothian Yeomanry (flails)

79th Assault Squadron, Royal Engineers (AVRE)

2nd Canadian Heavy Anti-aircraft Regiment

109th Heavy Anti-aircraft Regiment

2nd Army Group, Royal Canadian Artillery

3rd Army Group, Royal Artillery

4th Army Group, Royal Artillery

9th Army Group, Royal Artillery

19th Army Field Regiment (SP), Royal Canadian Artillery

GERMAN FORCES

I SS-PANZERKORPS

12.SS-Panzer-Division 'Hitlerjugend' (elements)

SS-Panzer-Regiment 12

SS-Panzergrenadier-Regiment 25

SS-Panzergrenadier-Regiment 26

SS-Panzerjäger-Abteilung 12

Divisional units

    Divisions-Begleit-Kompanie SS 12

    SS-Panzer-Aufklärungs-Abteilung 12

    SS-Aufklärungs-Gruppe Wienecke

    SS-Flak-Abteilung 12

    SS-Werfer-Abteilung 12

    SS-Artillerie-Regiment 12

89.Infanterie-Division

Grenadier-Regiment 1055

Grenadier-Regiment 1056

Artillerie-Regiment 189

Heeres-Artillerie-Abteilung (Mot.) 1151 (attached)

Heeres-Artillerie-Abteilung (Mot.) 1193 (attached)

Kampfgruppe, 85.Infanterie-Division (arriving from 9th)

Corps troops

schwere SS-Panzer-Abteilung 101

SS-Nachrichten-Abteilung 101

SS-Artillerie-Abteilung 101

SS-Vielfach-Werfer-Batterie 12

SS-Werfer-Abteilung 101

SS-Flak-Abteilung 101

Divisions-Begleit-Kompanie SS 101

Elements, schwere Panzerjäger-Abteilung (mot.) 1039

Elements, schwere Panzerjäger-Abteilung (mot.) 1053

Elements, Werfer-Regiment 83

OPPOSING PLANS

ALLIED

The execution of Totalize and the German forces' resistance to it owed much to either side's respective plans. The Allied planning for Totalize commenced on 30 July, when the 21st Army Group commander, General Bernard Montgomery, ordered Simonds to begin planning a new offensive towards Falaise, slated for around 10 days time. One of the key original purposes of this offensive was to support future operations that were going to be undertaken further to the west by the British Second Army. On 1 August Simonds produced an insightful outline appreciation of the situation in which this offensive was to be conducted. In good staff fashion, this appreciation simplified the situation into five succinct observations, from each of which he drew a logical deduction.

A group of Canadian staff officers meet, presumably for an 'Orders' group briefing, at some unidentified forward headquarters during the battle for Normandy. (Library and Archives Canada PA-116515)

His first observation was that the open terrain over which Totalize would be fought, which was dominated by enemy-held high ground to the south, rendered his forces highly vulnerable to the long-range lethality of concealed enemy tanks and anti-tank guns. From this he deduced that the proposed offensive would both have to secure the high ground and be mounted when enemy observation was restricted. He next observed that the enemy's defences comprised two separate lines. Therefore, he deduced, the planned operation would have to mount two separate break-in battles. Third, Simonds observed that previously during the Normandy campaign Allied offensive momentum had faltered just as it reached the depths of the German defensive zone due to diminishing artillery and aerial fire support. Simonds concluded that a proportion of the aerial fire support available for the planned offensive would have to be preserved for the second break-in attack.

In his fourth observation, Simonds noted that the slated offensive could not secure tactical surprise in terms of objectives or the axis of attack as these were obvious. Therefore, Simonds concluded, it was essential that the offensive achieved tactical surprise in terms of method and timing. Finally, Simonds observed that during the execution of this future offensive it would prove impractical to suppress all the enemy depth anti-tank assets for the entire amount of time required. Thus, he deduced the envisaged offensive would have to destroy these assets as it unfolded, rather than just suppress them. From this piece of staff work the entire corps plan for Totalize unfolded.

During the next three days Simonds and his staff worked feverishly to translate these five deductions into a coherent plan. Then, on 5 August, Simonds outlined to his senior officers his highly innovative corps plan. After heavy night bombers had struck five flank targets, two infantry divisions would mount the initial surprise night break-in using novel infiltration tactics; all-arms mobile column battle groups would bypass the enemy's village-based forward defences to penetrate the entire depth of the German position. These columns would overrun the enemy's anti-tank, rocket-launcher, artillery and mortar positions, secure key high ground and repel enemy counter-attacks. To ensure that the columns' infantry could keep up with the armour they would be embussed in troop-carrying vehicles. The corps also initiated various control measures to minimise the inevitable command and control degradation that would arise during night-time operations.

To maintain fire support for the second break-in battle (when only a few artillery pieces would still be in range), Simonds employed just half the available bombers to support his initial night assault, backed by all available artillery pieces; half the aerial bombers would remain available to support the second break-in battle timed for the early afternoon on D+1. During this second phase one armoured and one infantry division would break through this second enemy line; in the third, exploitation, phase two armoured divisions would advance south to seize the high ground located both north-north-west of Falaise (hills 180, 195 and 206) and north-east of that town (hills 170 and 155).

On 6 August Simonds' intelligence assets discerned that the opposing 1.SS-Panzer-Division Leibstandarte SS Adolf Hitler was withdrawing from the positions it

Allied armour moves forward during 7 August in preparation for the start of Totalize. (Library and Archives Canada PA-132904)

The revised II Canadian Corps plan, 6 August 1944.

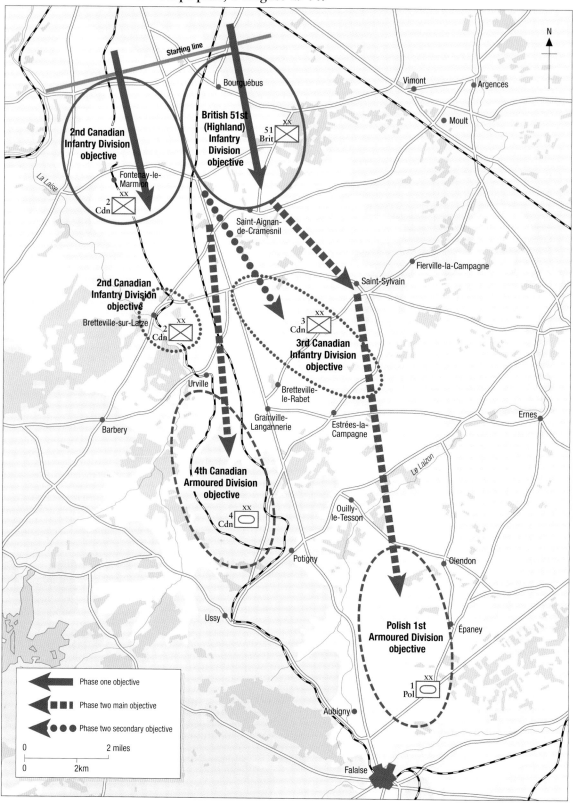

Starting line

Bourguébus

Vimont

Argences

Moult

2nd Canadian Infantry Division objective

British 51st (Highland) Infantry Division objective

51 Brit XX

Fontenay-le-Marmion

2 Cdn XX

La Laise

Saint-Aignan-de-Cramesnil

Fierville-la-Campagne

Saint-Sylvain

2nd Canadian Infantry Division objective

Bretteville-sur-Laize

2 Cdn XX

3 Cdn XX

3rd Canadian Infantry Division objective

Urville

Bretteville-le-Rabet

Ernes

Barbery

Grainville-Langannerie

Estrées-la-Campagne

Le Laizon

4th Canadian Armoured Division objective

4 Cdn XX

Ouilly-le-Tesson

Olendon

Potigny

Ussy

Polish 1st Armoured Division objective

Épaney

1 Pol XX

	Phase one objective
	Phase two main objective
	Phase two secondary objective

0 — 2 miles

0 — 2km

Aubigny

Falaise

28

occupied facing II Canadian Corps' front. His staff soon also ascertained that the 'Leibstandarte' was being replaced by the arriving 89.Infanterie-Division. The corps' Intelligence staff concluded that the 'Leibstandarte' was probably redeploying to bolster the enemy's reserve position. This deduction was incorrect, as the German high command had ordered the 'Leibstandarte' to rush westward to participate in the German counter-offensive at Mortain.

On hearing of the perceived redeployment of the 'Leibstandarte' from its current positions to the second defensive line, Simonds concluded that his initial break-in might prove easier and the second break-in more difficult than had been anticipated. On 6 August, therefore, he thus issued a modified corps plan. This, controversially, committed two armoured divisions to the second break-in battle; both commanders raised concerns over the narrow frontages allotted them, but Simonds refused to alter his plan. He also amalgamated the operation's second break-in and third (exploitation) phases into a new consolidated second phase; through exploiting any advantage accruing from the second bombing run, this aimed to generate greater forward momentum so that the high ground north of Falaise was secured by 9 August, earlier than previously anticipated.

In the final corps plan of 6 August the initial night break-in (Phase I) remained unchanged. From 2330hrs, 7 August, to the west of the south-south-east axis of the main Caen–Falaise road, Major-General Charles Foulkes' 2nd Canadian Infantry Division was to attack with 2nd Canadian Armoured Brigade under command. In the east Major-General Tom G. Rennie's 51st

The main and rear headquarters of the 4th Canadian Armoured Division consisted of eight main sections: the General Staff (Operations), Adjutant and Quartermaster-General, Artillery, Engineers, Signals, Medical, Supply and Ordnance branches.

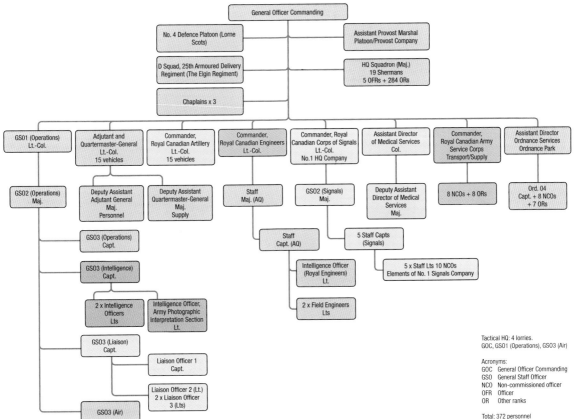

4th Canadian Armoured Division Main/Rear Headquarters

General Officer Commanding

No. 4 Defence Platoon (Lorne Scots)

D Squad, 25th Armoured Delivery Regiment (The Elgin Regiment)

Chaplains x 3

Assistant Provost Marshal Platoon/Provost Company

HQ Squadron (Maj.) 19 Shermans 5 OFRs + 284 ORs

GSO1 (Operations) Lt.-Col.

Adjutant and Quartermaster-General Lt.-Col. 15 vehicles

Commander, Royal Canadian Artillery Lt.-Col. 15 vehicles

Commander, Royal Canadian Engineers Lt.-Col.

Commander, Royal Canadian Corps of Signals Lt.-Col. No.1 HQ Company

Assistant Director of Medical Services Col.

Commander, Royal Canadian Army Service Corps Transport/Supply

Assistant Director Ordnance Services Ordnance Park

GSO2 (Operations) Maj.

Deputy Assistant Adjutant General Maj. Personnel

Deputy Assistant Quartermaster-General Maj. Supply

Staff Maj. (AQ)

GSO2 (Signals) Maj.

Deputy Assistant Director of Medical Services Maj.

8 NCOs + 8 ORs

Ord. 04 Capt. + 8 NCOs + 7 ORs

GSO3 (Operations) Capt.

Staff Capt. (AQ)

5 Staff Capts (Signals)

GSO3 (Intelligence) Capt.

Intelligence Officer (Royal Engineers) Lt.

5 x Staff Lts 10 NCOs Elements of No. 1 Signals Company

2 x Intelligence Officers Lts

Intelligence Officer, Army Photographic Interpretation Section Lt.

2 x Field Engineers Lts

GSO3 (Liaison) Capt.

Liaison Officer 1 Capt.

Liaison Officer 2 (Lt.) 2 x Liaison Officer 3 (Lts)

GSO3 (Air)

Tactical HQ: 4 lorries.
GOC, GSO1 (Operations), GSO3 (Air)

Acronyms:
GOC   General Officer Commanding
GSO   General Staff Officer
NCO   Non-commissioned officer
OFR   Officer
OR   Other ranks

Total: 372 personnel

(Highland) Infantry Division was to operate with the British 33rd Armoured Brigade under command. Both divisions' three lead (embussed) infantry battalions would link up with armoured forces and supporting arms to form three Canadian and three British mobile columns; Canadian reconnaissance assets also provided a seventh column. These seven all-arms battle groups would infiltrate between the German forward defended localities to seize key depth objectives located between 5,300m and 6,200m behind the front.

As this mobile column assault unfolded three Canadian and two British infantry battalions meanwhile would each attack on foot one of the enemy-defended localities that had been bypassed by the mobile column assault. By 1000hrs, 8 August, therefore, the two Allied divisions would have both secured a firm base within this 6,300m-deep, 5,400m-wide penetration of the German front, and subsequently repelled any immediate local enemy counter-attacks. To support this initial break-in heavy night bombers would strike five flank targets to suppress enemy enfilade fire, while 360 artillery pieces were to lay down a rolling barrage behind which the mobile columns would advance.

Totalize Phase II was to commence at 1400hrs, 8 August, after American heavy day bombers had struck six targets located along the second German defensive position. The 4th Canadian and Polish 1st Armoured divisions were then to strike south to penetrate this second German position, and subsequently generate significant offensive momentum. The 4th Canadian Armoured Division was to advance both down, and west of, the main Caen–Falaise road to secure the high ground north-west of Falaise (hills 180, 195, and 206) by the evening of 9 August. Simultaneously, to the east the Polish 1st Armoured Division would thrust south-south-east to secure the high ground north-east of Falaise (hills 170 and 155). Both divisions would thus dominate the lateral road through Falaise. To assist this advance, each division could request fire from on-call artillery concentrations from its organic field artillery regiments and an allocated Army Group, Royal Artillery. Simultaneously, the 2nd Canadian Infantry, 3rd Canadian Infantry and the British 51st (Highland) Infantry divisions were to secure subsidiary objectives on the flanks of the offensive.

Seated in the foreground, Sergeant E. Owen conducts an Orders (O-) Group for personnel of No.1 Protective Troop, Headquarters Squadron, 4th Canadian Armoured Brigade, at Vaucelles, on 7 August 1944. The briefing undoubtedly covered the brigade's move forward during the next morning to spearhead Totalize Phase II. (Library and Archives Canada PA-131363)

GERMAN

Simonds' Totalize plan was based on detailed intelligence on the opposing I SS-Panzerkorps, part of 5.Panzerarmee; Allied reading of enemy intentions from this information, however, was not entirely accurate. In early August the OBW still viewed I SS-Panzerkorps' sector along the Bourguébus Ridge south of Caen as the key 'hinge' that supported the still cohesive German front that stretched westward opposite the British Second Army to the Caumont area. The orders issued by OBW and 5.Panzerarmee to SS-Oberstgruppenführer Josef Dietrich insisted that his I SS-Panzerkorps mount a protracted, unyielding defence of its current front line along the Bourguébus Ridge.

However, at the same time as issuing these orders, OBW had begun the withdrawal of significant elements of I SS-Panzerkorps' armour, which were to rush westward to help with the counter-attacks intended to bolster the collapsing German front in the west opposite the American First Army. During 3–6 August, therefore, the 1.SS-Panzer-Division Leibstandarte SS Adolf Hitler, as well as a battle group from the 12.SS-Panzer-Division 'Hitlerjugend', redeployed from the I SS-Panzerkorps sector. The positions vacated by the former were taken over by the newly arrived 89.Infanterie-Division, while no reinforcements arrived to make good the loss of the 'Hitlerjugend' battle group. Thus while I SS-Panzerkorps' mission remained the same – unyielding defence of key terrain – by 7 August the forces available to achieve this task had been significantly diminished. Dietrich complained bitterly about the diminution of his key armoured reserves. In the operational climate of the collapse of the German front to the west, however, his complaints cut little ice with his superiors; they were desperately striving to gather enough armour to put in a desperate counter-attack towards Mortain to stem the deluge of American armour pouring into the interior of France.

The detailed I SS-Panzerkorps plan, therefore, remained that of mounting an intractable defence of the initial front-line defensive systems. This scheme envisaged that if Allied attacks secured penetrations of the front, hastily organised local armoured counter-attacks would repel such incursions. If such ripostes failed, Dietrich's defensive plan envisaged that a more deliberate larger-scale counter-attack would be mounted. This would be executed by the Panzergrenadiers of the 'Hitlerjugend', backed by the division's Panzer IVs and Panthers and possibly the Tigers of schwere SS-Panzer-Abteilung 101. Only after these deliberate ripostes had failed and the entire defensive position was on the point of being overwhelmed, would 5.Panzerarmee permit the front-line forces to mount a staged withdrawal back to the second German defensive position. There was no formal withdrawal plan for the worst-case scenario of the Allied attacks penetrating this second defensive line – for in the politicised atmosphere that flourished following the failed assassination attempt on Hitler, such 'defeatist' thinking was likely to lead a commander to be sacked.

Captain Frederick Tilston of the Essex Scottish Regiment having a cigarette break during the days before Totalize, 5 August 1944. On 1 March 1945, during the battle for the Rhineland, a wounded Tilston was awarded the Victoria Cross for conspicuous gallantry and steadfast determination in the face of fierce enemy resistance. (Library and Archives Canada PA-132827)

The I SS-Panzerkorps actual defensive system represented the physical manifestation of these defensive plans. The system comprised two main elements: the 6,300m-deep forward zone, which was based on the defence of 11 village localities; some 2,000m further south a partially prepared reserve position was under construction between Bretteville-sur-Laize and Saint-Sylvain. Up to 6 August the 'Leibstandarte' had occupied well-established defensive positions within this first line, stretching from the Orne River near May-sur-Orne in the west through to beyond La Hogue in the east; the front in this sector had changed little since the mid-July Goodwood offensive. However, during 3–6 August OBW redeployed the 'Leibstandarte' westward to support the Mortain counter-offensive. Its well-prepared positions were taken over by the newly arrived 89.Infanterie-Division.

Each of the 89.Infanterie-Division's two grenadier regiments deployed two of its battalions forward and the third as a reserve, according to usual German defensive practice. The division's four forward-deployed infantry battalions held a first line of seven village localities along the Bourguébus Ridge: running from west to east these were May-sur-Orne, Fontenay-le-Marmion, Verrières, Rocquancourt, Tilly-la-Campagne, Garcelles-Secqueville and La Hogue. By typical German standards, there was merely a thin belt of mines protecting the approaches to these forward positions. The German infantry were usually deployed in company strength in these villages, with platoons in foxholes and trenches dug in across the open fields between these villages. In most of these villages, the defenders enjoyed the support provided by several assault or self-propelled guns.

In addition, the two reserve battalions from the 89.Infanterie-Division's two grenadier regiments were deployed in depth holding a second line of four villages: from west to east Caillouet, Bretteville-sur-Laize, Saint-Aignan-de-Cramesnil and Cramesnil. The Germans had laid only a very small number of mines in front of these rear defended locations. The two reserve battalions protected the division's artillery firing positions but were also ready to launch immediate local counter-attacks to help restore the original front line as per standard German tactical doctrine. Finally, in the area of Bretteville-sur-Laize the 89.Infanterie-Division had deployed its fusilier battalion (a de-facto infantry battalion) as an additional reserve and counter-attack force.

Meanwhile, elements of the 'Hitlerjugend' division, acting as the corps' reserves, were deployed mainly to the south-west of the western end of the second German defensive positions, in the area west of Gouvix. By 7 August the only semi-prepared reserve German line was still very thinly held by just a few companies of infantry plus some anti-aircraft batteries from III Flakkorps. However, the 85.Infanterie-Division was in transit to join I SS-Panzerkorps and was slated to take up defensive positions along this reserve position when it arrived in a few days' time. Would this defensive layout prove capable of halting the surely inevitable resumption by II Canadian Corps of their offensive action southward from the Bourguébus Ridge sector?

Personnel of a Canadian armoured regiment sit on some spare Sherman tank track to read *The Maple Leaf* newspaper between Fleury-sur-Orne and Ifs during the prelude to Totalize. (Library and Archives Canada PA-162380)

THE CAMPAIGN

PHASE I: THE NIGHT INFILTRATION BREAK-IN BATTLE

During the late evening of 7 August, as darkness fell, the assault forces of the 2nd Canadian Infantry and the British 51st (Highland) Infantry divisions moved forward from their assembly areas south of Caen to their forming-up positions on the Totalize start-line between Saint-André-sur-Orne in the west and Soliers in the east. In the sector west of the main road the 2nd Canadian Infantry Division delegated conduct of the mobile column assault to the newly created ad-hoc 2nd Canadian Armoured Brigade Group, which was formed from the tactical marriage of the 2nd Canadian Armoured Brigade and the 4th Canadian Infantry Brigade; the experienced armoured commander Brigadier Robert Wyman remained in command of the Brigade Group for the entire mobile column night assault. The 2nd Canadian Infantry Division, however, maintained control of the overarching night assault, including the execution of the Canadian marching infantry assault mounted by the three battalions of 6th Canadian Infantry Brigade. In the eastern sector, the British 51st (Highland) Infantry Division and the British 33rd Armoured Brigade tactically co-operated in similar fashion to the Canadians, but without forming an ad-hoc brigade group to mount the column assault.

By 2300hrs, 7 August, the 2nd Canadian Armoured Brigade Group's four mobile columns had formed up ready to spearhead the night break-in assault in the western sector. The three columns of the 'triple column formation' formed up in close proximity to one another just west of Beauvoir Farm. Some 1,100m further east, near the main Caen–Falaise road, the fourth ('Recce') column assembled north-east of Troteval

View of the 'Churchill' Bailey bridge erected across the Orne during July 1944; many of the additional units brought forward for Totalize had headed south towards the front across this structure. (Library and Archives Canada PA-113679)

Final dispositions, 2330hrs, 7 August 1944.

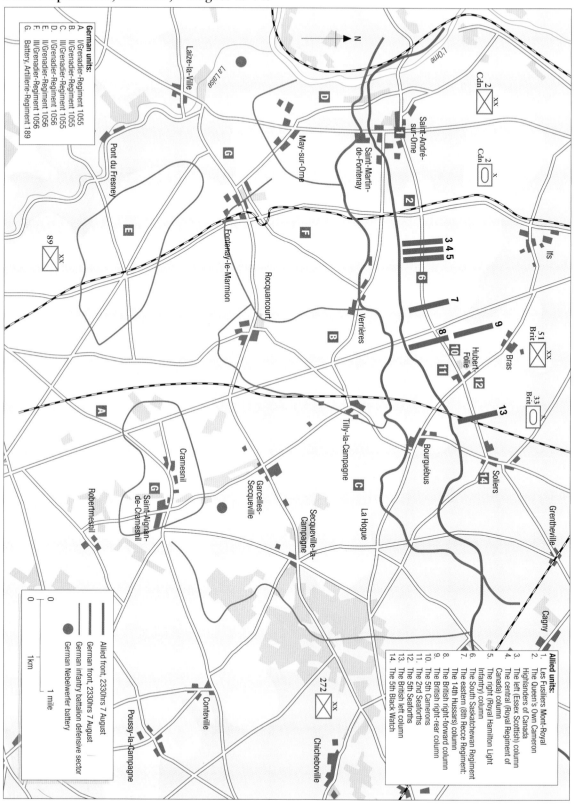

German units:
A. I/Grenadier-Regiment 1055
B. II/Grenadier-Regiment 1055
C. III/Grenadier-Regiment 1055
D. I/Grenadier-Regiment 1056
E. II/Grenadier-Regiment 1056
F. III/Grenadier-Regiment 1056
G. Battery, Artillerie-Regiment 189

Allied units:
1. Les Fusiliers Mont-Royal
2. The Queen's Own Cameron Highlanders of Canada
3. The left (Essex Scottish) column
4. The central (Royal Regiment of Canada) column
5. The right (Royal Hamilton Light Infantry) column
6. The South Saskatchewan Regiment
7. The eastern (8th Recce Regiment: The 14th Hussars) column
8. The British right-forward column
9. The British right-rear column
10. The 5th Camerons
11. The 2nd Seaforths
12. The 5th Seaforths
13. The British left column
14. The 5th Black Watch

Allied front, 2330hrs 7 August
German front, 2330hrs 7 August
German infantry battalion defensive sector
German Nebelwerfer battery

0   1km
0   1 mile

34

Farm. These columns were to rapidly infiltrate between the German defensive positions and (in the case of the triple formation) assemble at the designated debus area, before assaulting their objectives on foot. Simultaneously, 6th Canadian Infantry Brigade's three infantry battalions had respectively formed up north of Saint-Martin-de-Fontenay, just west of the triple column formation, and west of the eastern column ready to assault the enemy forward positions bypassed by these columns. The right-hand (Essex) column in the triple formation was to capture Caillouct, the central (Royals') column was to seize the north-western part of Hill 122, and the left-hand (Hamiltons') column was to secure both Les Carrières Quarry and Gaumesnil. These three columns were to advance 4,850m south-south-east to the fields of Pièce-de-Caillouet, where their infantry would debus from their carriers, march to their nearby objectives and then assault them. Simultaneously, the separate eastern (Recce) column

2nd Canadian Armoured Brigade Group

	Essex Scottish (Left)	Royal Regiment of Canada (Centre)	Royal Hamilton Light Infantry (Right)	14th Hussars (Eastern Column)
REAR		4 x Scout	Tactical HQ, 2nd Canadian Armoured Brigade	
		3 x Sherman 1 x Stuart		
		4 x Sherman	Tactical HQ, 4th Canadian Infantry Brigade	
		4 x Sherman		
		4 x Sherman		
		2 x Crusader: ARV		
		3 x Stuart (SHQ)		
Fortress Force		3 x Scout		
		3 x Sherman (RHQ)		
		4 x Sherman		
		4 x Sherman		
		4 x Sherman		
		2 x Crusader: ARV		4 x MMG UC
		3 x Stuart (SHQ)		4 x 6pdr ATG
		3 x Scout		4 x 6pdr ATG
		3 x Sherman (SHQ)		4 x TD
		4 x Sherman		3 x RV
		4 x Sherman		3 x RV
		4 x Sherman		3 x RV
Assault Force	4 x MMG UC	4 x MMG UC	4 x MMG UC	3 x RV
	4 x 17pdr ATG	4 x 17pdr ATG	4 x 17pdr ATG	3 x RV
	4 x 6pdr ATG	4 x 6pdr ATG	4 x 6pdr ATG	3 x RV
	4 x TD	4 x TD	4 x TD	3 x RV
	4 x TCV	4 x TCV	4 x TCV	3 x RV
	4 x TCV	4 x TCV	4 x TCV	3 x RV
	4 x TCV	4 x TCV	4 x TCV	3 x RV
	4 x TCV	4 x TCV	4 x TCV	3 x RV
	4 x TCV	4 x TCV	4 x TCV	3 x RV
	4 x TCV	4 x TCV	4 x TCV	3 x RV
	4 x TCV	4 x TCV	4 x TCV	3 x RV
	4 x TCV	4 x TCV	4 x TCV	3 x RV
	4 x TCV	4 x TCV	4 x TCV	3 x RV
	4 x TCV	4 x TCV	4 x TCV	3 x RV
Gapping Force	2 x Scout	2 x Scout	2 x Scout	2 x Scout
	4 x Sherman	4 x Sherman	4 x Sherman	4 x Sherman
	4 x Sherman	4 x Sherman	4 x Sherman	4 x Sherman
	4 x Sherman	4 x Sherman	4 x Sherman	4 x Sherman
	3 x AVRE	3 x AVRE	3 x AVRE	3 x AVRE
	3 x AVRE	3 x AVRE	3 x AVRE	3 x AVRE
	2 x Flail	2 x Flail	2 x Flail	2 x Flail
	4 x Flail	4 x Flail	4 x Flail	4 x Flail
	4 x Flail	4 x Flail	4 x Flail	4 x Flail
	4 x Sherman	4 x Sherman	4 x Sherman	4 x Sherman
	4 x Sherman	4 x Sherman	4 x Sherman	4 x Sherman
FRONT	1 x Sherman Nav ▼	1 x Sherman Nav ▼	1 x Sherman Nav ▼ Direction of advance	1 x Sherman Nav ▼

Acronyms:

ARV	Armoured reconnaissance vehicle
AVRE	Armoured Vehicle Royal Engineers
ATG	Anti-tank gun
MMG	Medium machine gun
RHQ	Regimental headquarters
SHQ	Squadron headquarters
RV	Reconnaissance vehicle
TCV	Troop carrying vehicle
TD	Tank destroyer
UC	Universal carrier

This diagram of the four Canadian mobile column formations depicts the types of vehicles in each row up to a depth of 47 rows. Each row had four, three or two vehicles. The vehicle types included Sherman tanks, Sherman flail tanks, troop-carrying vehicles, AVRE, Stuart light tanks, towed 6pdr anti-tank guns and towed 17pdr guns.

Brigadier Robert A. Wyman (right) shows Lieutenant-General Crerar a German oil container during the latter's visit to a Canadian officers' training course, January 1944. (Library and Archives Canada PA-136671)

would advance to secure the north-eastern part of Hill 122, where it would link up with the Royals' column. Meanwhile, 6th Canadian Infantry Brigade's three infantry battalions would assault on foot the four enemy-held villages outflanked by the columns: May-sur-Orne, Fontenay-le-Marmion, Verrières and Rocquancourt.

Meanwhile, around 2200hrs, the three British mobile columns had moved forward from their concentration areas located south of Caen around Cormelles to initiate the assault on the eastern sector. Moving south in movement corridors identified by engineer-placed lamps, by 2300hrs all three British columns had formed up in their designated starting positions. Organised in a similar manner to the Canadian phalanxes, each British column comprised an embussed infantry battalion from 154th Infantry Brigade, and an armoured regiment from 33rd Armoured Brigade, plus various supporting arms. The forward left British column, consisting of the embussed 1st Black Watch and the Shermans of the 1st Northamptonshire Yeomanry, formed up in the fields west-south-west of Soliers. Its mission was to advance 5,800m south-south-east to capture Saint-Aignan-de-Cramesnil and the adjacent orchards at Delle-de-la-Roque.

Simultaneously, the right-forward British column assembled near La Guinguette, just east of the main Caen–Falaise road. This column comprised the infantry of the 7th Argyll and Sutherland Highlanders plus the tanks of 144th Regiment, Royal Armoured Corps. The column's task was to advance 3,600m south-south-east and capture the village of Cramesnil, as well as the adjacent woodblocks and the nearby road intersection at Le Haut Bosq. Finally, deployed behind this unit was the British right-rear column, which was formed from the infantry of the 7th Black Watch and the Shermans of 148th Regiment, Royal Armoured Corps. Its mission was to advance 2,800m and secure Garcelles-Secqueville.

A Canadian Universal Carrier moves forward during 8 August 1944; note the sandbags that the crew have placed on the front of the vehicle to augment its armoured protection. (Library and Archives Canada PA-132656)

The Canadian triple column formation contained three mobile columns – in effect, multi-national task-oriented all-arms battle groups. Each column fielded an embussed 4th Canadian Infantry Brigade infantry battalion, two 2nd Canadian Armoured Brigade Sherman tank troops, a troop each of British Sherman flails and AVRE, a Canadian M10 tank destroyer troop, two Canadian anti-tank gun troops, a Canadian carrier-mounted medium machine-gun platoon and a Canadian engineering section. At the left-column's rear

came the 2nd and 4th Canadian Infantry brigades' tactical headquarters. The fourth (Recce) column comprised the division's 8th Reconnaissance Regiment (14th Canadian Hussars), rather than an infantry battalion, together with a Sherman squadron, and supporting arms as per the other columns. Each phalanx-like column thus comprised 100–140 vehicles organised into a dense formation with four vehicles abreast on a narrow 16m frontage and with a depth of up to 230m spread across 28–35 rows.

Columns of Allied Priest improvised armoured personnel carriers assemble near Caen on 7 August 1944, ready to initiate the surprise Totalize night break-in assault. (Library and Archives Canada PA-129172)

As the planning for Totalize unfolded, it became immediately apparent that the available numbers of M3 White scout cars, Universal Carriers, half-tracks and GMC armoured trucks allocated to embus the six infantry battalions allocated to the Phase I night-time mobile column assault would provide insufficient lift. Recognising this, on 31 July Simonds requested that surplus American-loaned Priest 105mm fully tracked SPGs, which had been used for the D-Day assault, be converted to improvised armoured APCs. Consequently, on 1 August Montgomery authorised the improvisation of the British/Canadian armies' first fully tracked APCs of World War II. An ad-hoc workshop codenamed 'Kangaroo' was created that same day using 250 personnel. In just 72 frenetic hours of non-stop activity between 3 and 6 August the workshop converted 76 Priest SPGs into improvised APCs through the removal of the main armament as well as other modifications. Running short of sheet metal to complete these modifications, Kangaroo personnel resorted to welding strips removed from damaged landing craft still languishing on the D-Day beaches, prompting an official protest from the Royal Navy, who still aimed to repair the craft. Each APC could carry a 10-man section of infantry, so the 76 Kangaroos converted provided the lift for an additional entire infantry battalion, making up the calculated shortfall in capacity. During 5–6 August the column infantry battalions participated in hurried training with these new APCs to develop appropriate tactics and doctrine.

The Totalize Phase I night assault was facilitated by two principal forms of fire support: heavy bomber strikes and a rolling artillery barrage. From 2300hrs, 7 August, some 1,020 RAF Bomber Command Lancaster and Halifax heavy bombers dropped their bombs onto five targets located on the offensive's flanks. However, the intense dust thrown up by the first strikes so

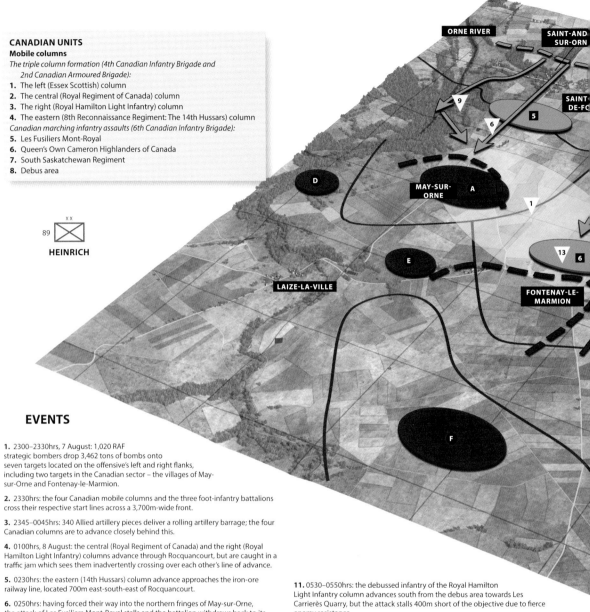

CANADIAN UNITS

Mobile columns

The triple column formation (4th Canadian Infantry Brigade and 2nd Canadian Armoured Brigade):
1. The left (Essex Scottish) column
2. The central (Royal Regiment of Canada) column
3. The right (Royal Hamilton Light Infantry) column
4. The eastern (8th Reconnaissance Regiment: The 14th Hussars) column

Canadian marching infantry assaults (6th Canadian Infantry Brigade):
5. Les Fusiliers Mont-Royal
6. Queen's Own Cameron Highlanders of Canada
7. South Saskatchewan Regiment
8. Debus area

89 ⊠ x x

HEINRICH

Map labels: ORNE RIVER · SAINT-AND SUR-ORN · SAINT-DE-FO · MAY-SUR-ORNE · LAIZE-LA-VILLE · FONTENAY-LE-MARMION

EVENTS

1. 2300–2330hrs, 7 August: 1,020 RAF strategic bombers drop 3,462 tons of bombs onto seven targets located on the offensive's left and right flanks, including two targets in the Canadian sector – the villages of May-sur-Orne and Fontenay-le-Marmion.

2. 2330hrs: the four Canadian mobile columns and the three foot-infantry battalions cross their respective start lines across a 3,700m-wide front.

3. 2345–0045hrs: 340 Allied artillery pieces deliver a rolling artillery barrage; the four Canadian columns are to advance closely behind this.

4. 0100hrs, 8 August: the central (Royal Regiment of Canada) and the right (Royal Hamilton Light Infantry) columns advance through Rocquancourt, but are caught in a traffic jam which sees them inadvertently crossing over each other's line of advance.

5. 0230hrs: the eastern (14th Hussars) column advance approaches the iron-ore railway line, located 700m east-south-east of Rocquancourt.

6. 0250hrs: having forced their way into the northern fringes of May-sur-Orne, the attack of Les Fusiliers Mont-Royal stalls and the battalion withdraws back to its starting positions near Saint-André-sur-Orne.

7. 0330–0400hrs: the advancing central (Royal Regiment of Canada) and the right (Royal Hamilton Light Infantry) columns reach the designated debus point at Pièce-de-Caillouet.

8. 0330hrs: the advance of the eastern (14th Hussars) column is stalled near the iron-ore railway line west of Lorguichon, some 1,200m short of their objective (the north-western fringes of Hill 122) by fierce enemy resistance.

9. 0415hrs: the attempted double assault on May-sur-Orne by Les Fusiliers Mont-Royal , which began at 0315hrs, stalls and the battalion withdraws north to its original starting positions for a second time.

10. 0520hrs: after reorganising, the central (Royal Regiment of Canada) column continues its advance to the north-eastern fringes of Hill 122 with its infantry still embussed.

11. 0530–0550hrs: the debussed infantry of the Royal Hamilton Light Infantry column advances south from the debus area towards Les Carrierès Quarry, but the attack stalls 400m short of the objective due to fierce enemy resistance.

12. 0600hrs: the remaining ten operational Priest APCs of the central (Royal Regiment of Canada) column mounts an improvised embussed assault on the north-eastern fringes of Hill 122, which is quickly secured. This is the first time that British rifle infantrymen from a standard infantry division mount an assault on an enemy position embussed in fully tracked armoured personnel carriers.

13. 0630hrs: the Queen's Own Cameron Highlanders of Canada secure the northern half of Fontenay-le-Marmion but fail to capture the southern half in the face of fierce local counter-attacks.

14. 0845–0915hrs: the stalled Essex Scottish column resumes its advance towards Caillouet but is then stymied by enemy tanks.

15. 0900–1000hrs: a mixed German tank and infantry force counter-attacks north along the main Caen–Falaise road towards the recently secured Canadian positions. The riposte is eventually driven back.

THE WESTERN (CANADIAN) SECTOR OF THE INITIAL TOTALIZE BREAK-IN BATTLE

The Allied and German dispositions at 2330hrs, 7 August, and the Allied advance and German counter-attacks through to 1000hrs, 8 August.

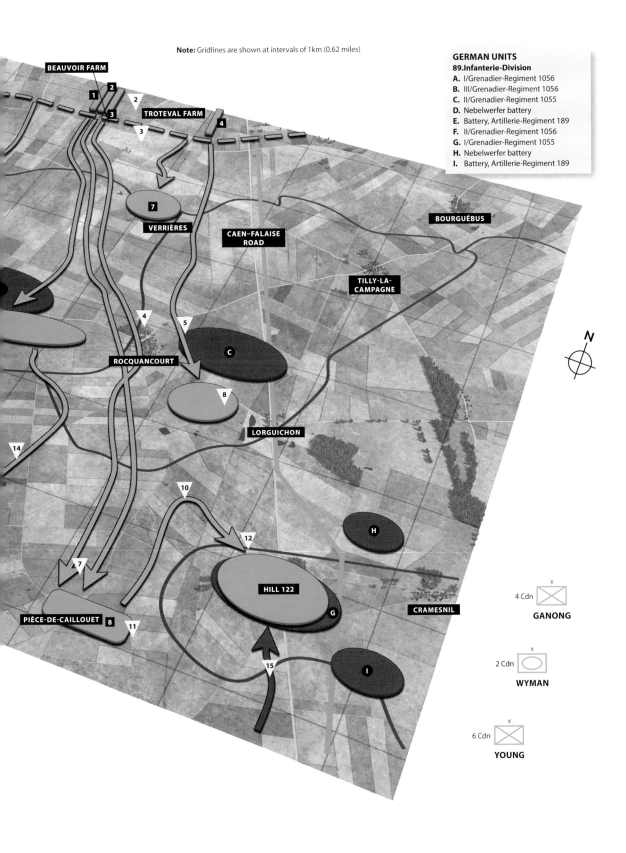

Note: Gridlines are shown at intervals of 1km (0.62 miles)

BEAUVOIR FARM

TROTEVAL FARM

GERMAN UNITS
89.Infanterie-Division
A. I/Grenadier-Regiment 1056
B. III/Grenadier-Regiment 1056
C. II/Grenadier-Regiment 1055
D. Nebelwerfer battery
E. Battery, Artillerie-Regiment 189
F. II/Grenadier-Regiment 1056
G. I/Grenadier-Regiment 1055
H. Nebelwerfer battery
I. Battery, Artillerie-Regiment 189

VERRIÈRES

CAEN–FALAISE
ROAD

BOURGUÉBUS

TILLY-LA-
CAMPAGNE

ROCQUANCOURT

LORGUICHON

CRAMESNIL

HILL 122

PIÈCE-DE-CAILLOUET

N

4 Cdn ⊠
GANONG

2 Cdn ⬭
WYMAN

6 Cdn ⊠
YOUNG

39

obscured these targets that 378 of the subsequent aircraft aborted their bomb drops. Consequently, only 3,492 tons of munitions were delivered. Next, the mobile column assault began at 2330hrs without the benefit of any preliminary bombardment, so as to maintain surprise. Subsequently, when the column advance reached the enemy front line, roughly 900m south of the start line, at 2345hrs, 340 Allied artillery pieces began delivering a rolling artillery barrage. These supporting fires ranged across a 4,600m frontage that covered the advance of all seven columns but not that of all the marching infantry assaults. Between 2345 and 0040hrs, 8 August, this barrage 'lifted' every 120 minutes, moving south-south-east in 180m stages, producing a roll forward at a pace of roughly 11km/h that extended to a depth of 4,700m. It was intended that the mobile columns would advance close behind this barrage, thus benefiting from its suppressive effect right up to and including their assaults on their respective final objectives.

The German dispositions

The initial German defensive front that the Allied forces assaulted at 2330hrs, 7 August, was manned by the recently arrived 89.Infanterie-Division. The division's Grenadier-Regiment 1056, led by Oberst Karl Roesler, held well-established positions in the sector west of the main Caen–Falaise road; its positions ran from the Orne River in the west through to Verrières in the east. Meanwhile the division's Grenadier-Regiment 1055 manned the front that stretched from Verrières east across the main road through to Bourguébus and beyond to a point north of La Hogue. This marked the right (eastern) flank of I SS-Panzerkorps' frontage; further east came the front held by 272. Infanterie-Division, controlled by the neighbouring corps command. The German front ran approximately west to east parallel to, but roughly 1,200m south of, the II Canadian Corps' start line.

The defenders deployed medium (bipod-mounted) and heavy (tripod-mounted) MG42 machine guns, together with anti-tank guns, to achieve overlapping fields of fire. Whilst the villages were each typically held by an infantry company supported by several forward-deployed anti-tank guns, the intervening open fields and copses were covered by rifle platoons in trenches. To augment the forward-deployed infantry platoons' organic fires (from MG42 medium machine guns and light mortars) elements from each infantry battalion's heavy company provided heavy mortars and MG42 heavy machine guns. Both grenadier regiments' heavy company, together with the divisional anti-tank battalion and a company from a corps-level self-propelled anti-tank gun battalion, provided additional anti-tank guns and infantry guns to stiffen the

The Orne River represented a substantial water obstacle and formed a natural geographical feature upon which to designate the north-western limits of operation for II Canadian Corps during Totalize; it would also provide economy of effort to have any exposed flank to the west defended along the line of this feature. (Author's collection)

forward defended locations. These deployments made these forward village strong points powerful ones that deployed considerable direct fires and mortar short-range indirect fires.

These forward defences were also supported by considerable long-range indirect fire assets. The Germans deployed these weapons across a U-shaped belt that ran south-east from Laize-la-Ville down to Bretteville-sur-Laize and back up north-east through Cintheaux up to Saint-Aignan-de-Cramesnil. These indirect-fire assets included the 89.Infanterie-Division's organic artillery, which comprised four batteries of 10.5cm leFH 18 light field howitzers and two batteries of 15cm sFH 18 heavy howitzers. I SS-Panzerkorps had also tactically allocated a number of independent army- and corps-level indirect fire units to bolster the 89.Infanterie-Division's supporting fires. These included two corps-level artillery battalions and a self-propelled howitzer battery. Finally, four batteries of Nebelwerfer rocket launchers were deployed in the 89.Infanterie-Division's sector, with firing positions located south-west of Fontenay-le-Marmion, west of Caillouet, south of Les Carrières Quarry, near Saint-Aignan-de-Cramesnil and north-east of Secqueville-la-Campagne.

The Canadian column advance commences

At 2330hrs, 7 August, the triple formation's three columns rumbled south-south-east past Beauvoir Farm towards the orchards north-west of Verrières in the face of initially light enemy fire; the night attack had caught the defenders by surprise. To help all seven mobile columns navigate effectively so as to stay on course as well as retain formational cohesion during their night advance, II Canadian Corps implemented various bespoke supporting measures. Bofors anti-aircraft guns fired tracer along the axes of advance that each column would follow while divisional signals units projected directional wireless beams along these axes. Moreover, each column's lead vehicle (which was responsible for navigation) had the position and bearing of its axis of advance fixed by a military survey unit. Furthermore, searchlights projected diffused illumination above the columns to lighten the night's shroud of darkness while field artillery fired green marker shells onto Hill 122, the objective for two of the columns. Finally in each columns' vanguard (termed Gapping Force) engineers pulled on armoured sledges by the troop of AVRE laid out tape and placed lights every 140m to assist the following vehicles in keeping on track.

At 2345hrs, with the triple column formation having closed on Verrières, 360 Allied artillery pieces initiated the rolling barrage. The three Canadian columns advanced south-south-east towards Rocquancourt following the barrage as it

On the walls of a typical Norman stone building in the hamlet of Verrières, a small plaque has been erected to commemorate the locality's liberation on 8 August by Canadian troops. (Author's collection)

THE CANADIAN TRIPLE COLUMN FORMATION ADVANCES FROM THE TOTALIZE START LINE NEAR BEAUVOIR FARM, 2330HRS, 7 AUGUST (PP. 42–43)

This view is taken from the perspective of the German infantrymen in their foxholes amid the fallow fields just south of Beauvoir Farm **(1)**. It is night-time, but the Allies are bouncing numerous searchlights off the low cloud to provide 'artificial moonlight' illumination, thus ensuring reasonable visibility for the columns.

The German infantrymen **(2)** can see a mass of Canadian armour advancing towards them. They are looking west-north-west towards the enemy tanks, organised in densely packed formations. Both soldiers shown here are firing white tracer with their K98 rifles **(3)** at the front rows of the tanks bearing down on them.

The Canadian columns are advancing south-south-east towards the German infantry. The two columns shown here – central **(4)** and eastern **(5)** (the western column being out of view to the left) – are in rows that occupy a mere 16m-wide frontage, four tanks per row, packed in phalanx-like formation. Just 3m separates each row of tanks. Most of the tanks are the standard M4A1 Sherman V **(6)**, with short-barrelled guns. The rest comprise the up-gunned Sherman Firefly, with its distinctive long barrel and muzzle brake **(7)**. The tanks are kicking up dust as they advance across the dry fields. At the head of each column is a solitary navigating standard Sherman V **(8)**.

lifted away from them. This dense phalanx of 550 armoured vehicles threw up such dense and extensive dust clouds as they traversed the dry ground that this overwhelmed the Allied illumination efforts designed to aid navigation. The columns found it increasingly difficult to stay on course and retain formation cohesion in the dust-reinforced darkness. This forced the three columns to halt frequently to re-orientate themselves and regroup, which meant that they soon fell behind the barrage as the latter lifted south according to its pre-arranged schedule. The triple column formation thus lost much of the suppressive benefit that the barrage was designed to produce so as to aid the columns in their advance.

As the triple column formation approached Rocquancourt, the western (Essex) column experienced particularly severe problems in maintaining formational cohesion. It also encountered accurate enemy direct fire from several anti-tank guns deployed forward to support the infantry platoon that defended Rocquancourt. By 0105hrs the Essex column had lost all cohesion, with numerous vehicles having blundered in the darkness away from the dwindling main body. The remnants of the column halted some 1,100m west of Rocquancourt to regroup. It took several hours for scouts to locate the column's scattered vehicles and bring them back in to re-form the phalanx.

Meanwhile, the central (Royals') and eastern (Hamiltons') columns of the Canadian triple column formation had struggled on despite both experiencing increasing fragmentation and having lost the artillery barrage. At 0110hrs they neared Rocquancourt in the face of increasing enemy fire. However, the two disorientated columns failed to bypass the village as planned. Instead they blundered into both the village and one another, creating a major traffic jam with 350 vehicles jostling for room for manoeuvre within the already cluttered narrow streets of Rocquancourt. By now enemy resistance had also picked up and the ensuing defensive fires knocked out several Canadian vehicles, making movement through the narrow streets even more difficult. Eventually, around 0140hrs the central (Royals') column managed to extricate itself from the jam by detouring east of Rocquancourt; this thus reversed the planned axes of advance of the central and eastern columns. Finally, by 0150hrs both the Royals' and Hamiltons' columns had managed to emerge onto several narrow farm tracks that ran south beyond Rocquancourt's southern fringes.

As the Canadian triple column formation rumbled south-south-east during the first hours of Totalize Phase I, some 800m further east the final Canadian mobile formation – the eastern (Recce) column – had also began its advance south-south-east from Troteval Farm towards the northern fringes of Hill 122. Passing east of Verrières by 2345hrs, the advancing Recce column picked up the rolling artillery barrage. Subsequently, the column passed north-east of the village of Rocquancourt heading for the hamlet of Lorguichon, thus avoiding the jam caused in the former village by the advance of the Royals' and Hamiltons' columns. By 0125hrs the Recce column had reached the bridge by which the Rocquancourt–Lorguichon road crossed over the north–south route of the iron-ore railway; this location was just 180m short of the main Caen–Falaise road.

The British column advance begins

At 2330hrs, across the sector east of the main Caen–Falaise road, the assault of the three British mobile columns commenced at the same time as that mounted by the Canadian columns to the west. Two British formations – the right-forward and right-rear columns – formed up on the western flank of the 51st (Highland) Infantry Division sector, close to the eastern side of the Caen–Falaise road. The final British mobile formation – the left column – formed-up some 1,500m further east close to Soliers. The missions of the British right-forward, right-rear and left columns were, respectively, to capture the villages and surrounding environs of Cramesnil, Garcelles-Secqueville and Saint-Aignan-de-Cramesnil.

The 140 vehicles of the right-forward British column set off promptly at 2330hrs from near La Guinguette, just east of the main Caen–Falaise road, and slowly headed south through the darkness towards the German front. The Sherman tanks of the 144th Regiment, RAC led the column, behind which followed the ranks of Kangaroo APCs, Universal Carriers and scout cars that carried the infantry of the 7th Argyll and Sutherland Highlanders. Deployed behind them, however, the vehicles of the right-rear British column had to wait patiently for 15 minutes to allow the rearward vehicles of the column in front of them to cross the start line. Finally, at 2345hrs the vehicles of the right-rear column began to roll forward along the same axis of advance. Just as in the Canadian sector, the movement at night of 280 vehicles across bone-dry fields kicked up far more dust than had been anticipated; this masked the illumination measures adopted to assist the columns. As early as 0030hrs, 8 August, both British right columns had already consequently found navigation and the retention of column cohesion incredibly difficult as their vehicles pushed south through the enemy lines.

Meanwhile at 2330hrs, 7 August, the 145 vehicles of the British left column moved forward across the corps start line from their positions located just north of the Hubert-Folie–Soliers road, to the west of the village of Soliers. The column's task was to advance 5,700m south-south-east, bypassing German-held Tilly-la-Campagne, to capture Saint-Aignan-de-Cramesnil and the wooded high ground just to the south. The column was led by two troops of Sherman flails from the 1st Lothians plus the standard Sherman battle tanks of Lieutenant-Colonel Doug Forster's 1st Northamptonshire Yeomanry. Behind this spearhead force, the bulk of the left column's remaining rows comprised the troop-carrying vehicles (TCVs) in which the infantry of Lieutenant-Colonel John Hopwood's 1st Black Watch were embussed. As with the other British columns, the armoured commander – in this case Forster – led the column during the movement phase. Rumbling forward on a south-south-east axis, at 2335hrs the column's vehicles reached Les Fresnes and passed across the north–south route of the iron-ore railway via the gap in the embankment. Then, at 2345hrs, the Allied rolling artillery barrage began just as the column approached the village of Bourguébus. Subsequently, the column's leading Sherman flails struggled to cross two steep-sided sunken lanes located south-south-west of Bourguébus; the ensuing 10-minute delay meant that the left column had fallen behind the southward movement of the barrage. Just as with the Canadian columns, by 0030hrs, 8 August, any benefit to be accrued by Forster's left column from the artillery barrage's suppressive effect on the enemy was lost due to the latter's fixed progression southward.

The Canadian column assaults

By 0150hrs, 8 August, therefore, all four Canadian mobile columns had successfully covered half the distance to their objectives. By that time the lead component in the triple column formation, the Royals' column, had emerged south out of Rocquancourt and was moving south-south-east following a track. The column was making steady progress covering the remaining 2,100m to the designated debus area in the fields of Pièce-de-Caillouet, located 1,100m north-west of the hamlet of Gaumesnil. This track's axis ran south-south-east to the west of the north–south route of the single-track iron-ore railway line. Following behind the rather dispersed Royals' formation, the even more fragmented Hamiltons' column also advanced south-south-east using the same track as the Royals, but also several tracks located further west.

At 0205hrs, the first elements of the Royals' column reached the debus area, with the remaining elements arriving over the next 55 minutes; during this time various elements of the Hamiltons' formation reached the debus area. Both columns had reached the Pièce-de-Caillouet debus area much later than planned, as the barrage had already lifted further south some 100 minutes previously. In retrospect the Allied command's anticipated rate of advance for the Canadian columns (as indicated by the rate at which the barrage lifted south) was over-optimistic, given the inevitable chaos of night-time operations. Subsequently, between 0205 and 0500hrs both columns spent far longer than planned at the debus area: they gathered in fragments of their formations and single isolated vehicles that had become detached in the darkness from their main bodies and reorganised themselves ready for the next (assault) phase of the mission. As planned, after the completion of the movement phase of the mobile column attack, command reverted from each column's senior armoured leader to the infantry commanding officer for the assault phase.

Table 1: command and control

	Move to debus area	Assault on objectives
Overall command 2nd Canadian Armoured Brigade Group	Command 2nd Canadian Armoured Brigade (Wyman)	Command 2nd Canadian Armoured Brigade (Wyman)
Gapping Force (overall)	Commanding officer Sherman Regiment (Sherbrooke Fusiliers)	n/a
Assault Force (overall)	Command 4th Canadian Infantry Brigade (Ganong)	Command 4th Canadian Infantry Brigade (Ganong)
Assault Force (Essex Scottish)	Senior Sherman troop command	Commanding officer Essex Scottish
Assault Force (Royal Regiment of Canada)	Senior Sherman troop command	Commanding officer Royal Regiment of Canada
Assault Force (Essex Scottish)	Senior Sherman troop command	Commanding officer Royal Hamilton Light Infantry
14th Hussars column (complete)	Commanding officer 14th Hussars	Commanding officer 14th Hussars

Command responsibility within the four column formations was broken down into two phases: the movement phase up to the debus point, and subsequently the actual assault onto the objective.

By the time that these two Canadian columns had reached the debus area, they had successfully passed right through the defensive positions manned by elements of the III battalions of both the Grenadier-Regiment 1055 and 1056. The columns had now reached the sector held by the 89.Infanterie-Division's western deployed reserve battalion, II/Grenadier-Regiment 1055. The locations held by this battalion included the position at Caillouet, probably held in company strength, which was the objective of the Essex column. The 89.Infanterie-Division's eastern deployed reserve battalion, the I/1055th Regiment, defended the sector along and east of the main Caen–Falaise road, including the key ground of Hill 122 (which was the objective for both the Royals' and Recce columns). The battalion had established company-strength positions around Hill 122, Saint-Aignan-de-Cramesnil and Cramesnil. After providing the defenders with supporting fires, it also seems that prior to daylight the division artillery elements that had been deployed in the woods south of Saint-Aignan-de-Cramesnil had withdrawn further to their south to avoid being overrun.

Around 0400hrs the new commander of the Royals' column, the experienced infanteer Lieutenant-Colonel J. C. H. Anderson, was busy reviewing the plan handed down to him by 2nd Canadian Armoured Brigade Group. Anderson was concerned about the delay in commencing the final movement to reach the objectives; with daylight rapidly approaching, and without the suppressive effect on the enemy provided by the barrage, Anderson was worried that heavy casualties might arise during their assault on the north-western fringes of Hill 122. To save time, Anderson ordered his infantry to re-embus in their TCVs; the entire column would proceed towards the objective with the infantry still embussed, rather than having the infantry march to their forming-up point for their assault on Hill 122.

Around 0500hrs the Royals' column, with infantry re-embussed, headed north as planned some 500m up the western side of the nearby embanked iron-ore railway to a spot where there was a gap in the embankment. The original plan envisaged that the column, including the debussed infantry, would pass through this gap before the infantry, supported by Sherman fire from the rear, assaulted north-east to secure the objective, Hill 122. In the darkness, however, the column fell victim of the 'fog of war' – it somehow failed to locate the gap in the railway embankment. Anderson quickly had to improvise a new plan, and ordered the column to detour north along the embankment's western face until it found another gap. After advancing north for a further 950m towards the farm at La Guerre, the column found that the embankment had dwindled away. Crossing eastward across the railway line the column headed 140m south-west and halted in the fields of Longues Rayes.

It was now 0540hrs, and the further delay caused by this detour again forced Anderson to improvise a new plan; he knew that his troops would incur greater casualties if they attacked in daylight, which was almost upon them. Instead of striking on foot north-east from the gap in the embankment as originally planned, Anderson ordered that the column's remaining carriers, with the infantry still embussed, would from their current positions in Longues Rayes charge guns blazing 800m east-south-east across the main road and onto Hill 122, their objective. Here the infantry would debus and then, as the Shermans provided fire support from the rear, they would overwhelm any enemy resistance to capture this dominating high ground.

At 0600hrs what was left of the fragmented column – ten of the 12 remaining Priest Kangaroo APCs

An Allied Priest self-propelled howitzer moves forward during the assault on the Gothic Line in Italy during late August 1944; this was the vehicle that II Canadian Corps converted to an improvised, fully tracked APC by removing its main armament. (Library and Archives Canada PA-184998)

carrying two Royals infantry companies – stormed uphill through the emerging daylight onto the north-western fringes of Hill 122, where they disgorged their soldiers; in the background the remaining Shermans rained high-explosive rounds down upon the enemy positions. During the next 25 minutes the Canadian infantry secured the hill after encountering only German small-arms fire. Given the strategic importance of Hill 122, the relative weakness of this German position seems surprising. Next, the Royals dispatched link men to locate the Canadian Recce column, which in the meantime was supposed to have secured the north-eastern fringes of Hill 122. The Royals failed to locate any elements of the Recce column. What the Royals did not know was that, having reached the road bridge over the iron-ore railway line located east-south-east of Rocquancourt, the Recce column's advance had been stalled by intense enemy resistance; the column had thus gone over to the defensive some 1,100m short of Hill 122.

From 0630hrs the rest of the Royals' column joined the infantry on Hill 122 and the troops began frantically to dig in, anticipating that the Germans would mount an immediate counter-attack to regain this vital high ground. Despite the rigid plan dictated from above, the Royals' commander had swiftly improvised in response to the inevitable friction of war. Through necessity Anderson embraced an innovative tactical approach utilising an improvised new vehicle, in so doing ensuring mission success. More than that, however, he also unleashed the first ever assault by British/Canadian rifle infantry mounted on fully tracked APCs – before the tactical doctrine for this had been developed.

Meanwhile, back at 0220hrs the first elements of the Hamiltons' column had begun arriving at the debus area, although it would take another 100 minutes for the majority of the formation to arrive. Undertaking the tasks of reorganising, regrouping and briefing subordinates on the assault plan also took the Hamiltons' column longer than anticipated. This meant that the infanteers were not ready to commence the final part of their mission to capture Les Carrières Quarry and Gaumesnil until 0520hrs. The riflemen of the Hamiltons advanced on foot south across the open fields located south of the debus area, with the Shermans moving forward to their rear. By 0530hrs, as the infantry closed on their objective, they were met by a hail of enemy defensive fire. Forward momentum was soon lost and the infantry became pinned down in the open fields, where they frantically dug shallow

View from the German defensive positions on Hill 122, looking north-west. Around 0600hrs on 8 August the ten remaining Priest APCs of the Royals' column charged machine-guns blazing towards the viewer from the fields of Longues Rayes in front of the wooden pole in the centre of the photograph. (Author's collection)

shell-scrapes. The arrival of daylight made the prospect of further progress even less likely, so the Canadian infantry established a defensive perimeter some 180m north of their objective, the quarry.

While the Royals' and Hamiltons' columns respectively fought their way onto, or near to, their designated objectives, the badly fragmented Essex Scottish column remained stalled west of Rocquancourt until 0845hrs by a combination of enemy fire and the need to reorganise. Next, the column advanced south along an axis 870m west of the route taken by the Royals' column until it halted 890m short of the village of Caillouet after spotting four enemy tanks deployed around the hamlet. Consequently, it was not until 1100hrs – after the enemy tanks had withdrawn – that the column assaulted Caillouet.

Once again, as the column was already many hours behind its intended schedule, the Essex Scottish commanding officer decided to improvise an innovative new assault plan for this unanticipated daylight assault on Caillouet. Almost certainly completely ignorant of the events on Hill 122, the Essex Scottish commander developed a plan remarkably similar to that improvised by Anderson of the Royals. As supporting fire from artillery, tanks and the machine guns on some rearward-deployed Priests suppressed the enemy, the column's remaining carriers rushed the infantry into Caillouet where they debussed, in what was the second Anglo-Canadian fully tracked APC-mounted assault of the war. Within an hour of fierce hand-to-hand combat the Canadian infantry had secured the village of Caillouet.

The British column assaults

As the Canadian columns mounted their assaults on their objectives west of the main Caen–Falaise road, a similar story unfolded in the British sector east of the main road. This narrative had left the British columns back at 0030hrs struggling to maintain column cohesion as they advanced between the initial enemy defensive positions. Around 0200hrs, after covering 2,200m, the now dispersed elements of the British right-forward column tried to cross over to the east of the iron-ore railway line at the level crossing at Point 84. As they did so the column encountered accurate German anti-tank fire as well as enemy infantry equipped with Panzerfaust launchers. Once this opposition had been suppressed, the increasingly dispersed column crossed the open fields of Le Laumel. By around 0400hrs the dispersed right-forward column had bypassed Lorguichon Woods to the west, and had closed on their objective, the hamlet of Cramesnil.

Meanwhile, back at 0040hrs Lieutenant-Colonel Forster's British left column was advancing south-south-east beyond Bourguébus across the open fields of Le Clos Neuf when it encountered accurate enemy fire delivered from the village of Tilly-la-Campagne, located to the south-west. Next, while slowly moving 1,450m south-south-east across the fields of Delle-du-Chemin-de-Secqueville to bypass Tilly, Forster's column continued to disintegrate as vehicles became disorientated in the dust-enriched darkness. In the face of intermittently fierce German defensive fire, which knocked out two Priest APCs, Forster's increasingly dissipated column continued to advance south-south-east, thus bypassing the German-held village of Garcelles-Secqueville to their east (which was to be secured by the British right-rear column).

Eventually, at 0240hrs the lead elements of Forster's British left column reached the designated debus area. This was the area immediately north of a thick and tall, gully-lined, tree-hedge line (identified by aerial photography) that ran west to east across the fields of Le Castelet. This thick hedge had been selected as the southern edge of the British left column's debus area not just because it was believed that the column's vehicles would struggle to get through it but also because it offered the TCVs some protection from enemy fire once the infantry had debussed from them. Fortuitously, Forster's column discovered several large man-made gaps in the hedge – presumably made recently by the enemy – and this permitted the column's armoured vehicles to move a further 750m south-south-east until they reached the thick tree-hedge line located a mere 275m north of Saint-Aignan-de-Cramesnil. Two British infantry companies debussed from their Priest APCs and began to move south towards their objective; meanwhile the Sherman tanks forced their way through several gaps in this second hedge and engaged the enemy forces that defended Saint-Aignan-de-Cramesnil.

Next, at 0345hrs, after the recently initiated Allied artillery concentration on Saint-Aignan-de-Cramesnil had ceased, the British infantry stormed the village while the Shermans poured fire into the enemy's defensive positions. A bitter and bloody hand-to-hand struggle for the village then ensued, during which both sides experienced several dozen casualties. After about 45 minutes of raging combat, however, the defenders began a gradual fighting withdrawal south out of the village. By around 0415hrs the Black Watch had secured the village and had marched 38 enemy prisoners back towards the Allied rear lines. The entire night advance had cost Forster's British left column 12 killed and 59 wounded or missing. Over the next three hours, as dense mists descended, the British infantry frantically dug in, while the tanks took up defensive positions; everyone peered fearfully south through the mists, straining to detect the first signs of the anticipated immediate German local counter-attack.

The Canadian infantry assaults

As the 2nd Canadian Division's four mobile columns advanced during the night of 7/8 August, its plan envisaged that the 6th Canadian Infantry Brigade's three battalions would attack on foot the German forward defended localities bypassed by the columns. On the corps' extreme right (west) the Francophone Les Fusiliers Mont-Royal were to capture the village of May-sur-Orne.

A soldier from Les Fusiliers Mont-Royal walks through the devastated village of May-sur-Orne on 9 August 1944. (Library and Archives Canada PA-132961)

Simultaneously the Queen's Own Cameron Highlanders of Canada would attack on an axis west of the triple column formation to secure the village of Fontenay-le-Marmion. Finally, operating on an axis between that of the triple column formation and the Canadian Recce column, the South Saskatchewan Regiment would capture first Verrières and then Rocquancourt. Two of these marching infantry assaults did not enjoy the support of the rolling barrage, with only the Saskatchewans being in the rectangular area of its fire. Les Fusiliers, however, did benefit from aerial fire support; the village of May-sur-Orne was one of five

THE ROYAL REGIMENT OF CANADA EMBUSSED IN PRIEST KANGAROO APCS ASSAULTS HILL 122, 0540HRS, 8 AUGUST (PP. 52–53)

This view is taken from the perspective of a group of German infantrymen in separate foxholes on the grassy north-western fringes of Hill 122 adjacent to (and east of) the main Caen–Falaise road **(1)**. Behind the advancing APCs can be seen Point 90 **(2)**, some 825m distant at the foot of the tall post. The 1944 Caen–Falaise road was considerably narrower than its modern counterpart, and was unmetalled. In the background can also be seen the spire of Rocquancourt church **(3)** and the railway embankment **(4)**.

Ten Canadian Priest Kangaroo armoured personnel carriers (APCs) **(5)** are heading towards the German position, their machine guns firing. The APCs are in two rows of five, with each row spread out over an 80m frontage. The lead row is rapidly closing in on the German positions, with the second row some 15m behind them. The Priest Kangaroo was a converted M7 105mm howitzer SPG with its gun removed (and a plate welded across the gap) and some internal features in the open-topped fighting compartment removed to make space for infantrymen. The markings on these APCs are those of the 13th Field Regiment of the 3rd Canadian Infantry Division.

Each APC carries 10 Canadian infanteers, who are keeping low and firing their Lee-Enfield No. 4 Mk. 1 rifles. The Royals' action at Hill 122 comprised the first APC-mounted infantry assault of the war. The German infantrymen, dug in waist deep in their foxholes, return fire with their K98 rifles **(6)**.

targets struck by RAF Bomber Command heavy bombers from 2300hrs, 7 August. None of the infantry attacks were to be supported by tanks. Given that all four locations would have been outflanked by a successful mobile column assault, II Canadian Corps did not expect the garrisons to stand and fight determinedly; this also explains why the marching infantry battalions were not allocated significant levels of direct and indirect fire support. Would the unfolding development of these actions validate Simonds' expectation that they would be relatively straightforward missions?

Deployed on II Canadian Corps' extreme western flank, Colonel Guy Gauvreau's Les Fusiliers Mont-Royal were to secure the vulnerable sector that bordered the Orne River. Les Fusiliers' mission was to strike south down the road from Saint-André-sur-Orne and Saint-Martin-de-Fontenay to capture May-sur-Orne. Facing Les Fusiliers were elements of I/Grenadier-Regiment 1056. At 2300hrs the lead Lancasters and Halifaxes dropped their bombs on targets in and around May-sur-Orne, which Allied artillery had identified with coloured smoke rounds. The intense clouds of dust generated by the initial bombing runs, however, so reduced visibility over the target that the rear squadrons either abandoned their missions rather than risk friendly fire accidents or else inaccurately dropped their bombs blind; subsequent assessments revealed that many bombs missed the German positions.

At 2355hrs Les Fusiliers attacked south from the Saint-André-sur-Orne crossroads down the north–south route of the road towards May-sur-Orne supported only by the fire of some 4.2in. heavy mortars. Over the next 100 minutes Les Fusiliers' B and C companies gradually advanced southward in the face of withering enemy artillery and machine-gun fire until they had become pinned down and dispersed just 320m short of the village after suffering heavy casualties. At 0255hrs, therefore, Gauvreau realised that his attack had stalled irrevocably. He now withdrew his forces and reorganised them to execute a new attack plan.

A mortar control team in action, 8 August 1944. One officer observes the accuracy of the fall of supporting mortar fire while the other communicates to the mortar crews via field telephone to correct their targeting. (Library and Archives Canada PA-131356)

At 0320hrs A and B companies resumed the frontal assault on the village to fix the enemy's attention; simultaneously the depleted C Company, together with D Company, attempted to infiltrate silently through the quarry ravine located west of the village and into May-sur-Orne itself. By 0335hrs, the infiltrators had managed to move undetected south-westward to the bottom of the ravine adjacent to the Orne River. During the next 25 minutes, while one group of infanteers scrambled east-south-east up the ravine, other groups of Canadian riflemen infiltrated through the ravine's wooded northern and southern shoulders towards the western fringes of the village. By 0400hrs the infiltrators had reached the top lip of the ravine just short of the village's western fringes. Suddenly the Germans spotted the Canadians and unleashed intense

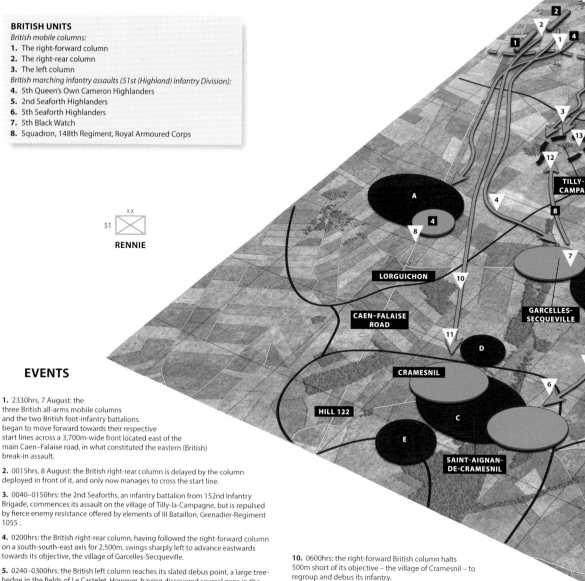

BRITISH UNITS

British mobile columns:
1. The right-forward column
2. The right-rear column
3. The left column

British marching infantry assaults (51st (Highland) Infantry Division):
4. 5th Queen's Own Cameron Highlanders
5. 2nd Seaforth Highlanders
6. 5th Seaforth Highlanders
7. 5th Black Watch
8. Squadron, 148th Regiment, Royal Armoured Corps

51 ⊠ XX
RENNIE

Map labels: **2**, **2**, **1**, **1**, **4**, **3**, **13**, **12**, **TILLY-L[A]-CAMPA[GNE]**, **A**, **4**, **8**, **4**, **8**, **7**, **LORGUICHON**, **10**, **CAEN–FALAISE ROAD**, **GARCELLES-SECQUEVILLE**, **11**, **D**, **5**, **CRAMESNIL**, **6**, **HILL 122**, **C**, **E**, **SAINT-AIGNAN-DE-CRAMESNIL**

EVENTS

1. 2330hrs, 7 August: the three British all-arms mobile columns and the two British foot-infantry battalions began to move forward towards their respective start lines across a 3,700m-wide front located east of the main Caen–Falaise road, in what constituted the eastern (British) break-in assault.

2. 0015hrs, 8 August: the British right-rear column is delayed by the column deployed in front of it, and only now manages to cross the start line.

3. 0040–0150hrs: the 2nd Seaforths, an infantry battalion from 152nd Infantry Brigade, commences its assault on the village of Tilly-la-Campagne, but is repulsed by fierce enemy resistance offered by elements of III Bataillon, Grenadier-Regiment 1055 .

4. 0200hrs: the British right-rear column, having followed the right-forward column on a south-south-east axis for 2,500m, swings sharply left to advance eastwards towards its objective, the village of Garcelles-Secqueville.

5. 0240–0300hrs: the British left column reaches its slated debus point, a large tree-hedge in the fields of Le Castelet. However, having discovered several gaps in the hedge presumably made by German tanks, the column continues to advance south with its infantry still embussed in Priest APCs and other TCVs towards the objective, the village of Saint-Aignan-de-Cramesnil.

6. 0345–0430hrs: the infantry of the British left column (the 1st Black Watch) supported by the Shermans of the 1st Northamptonshire Yeomanry assault and secure the village of Saint-Aignan-de-Cramesnil.

7. 0430–0530hrs: the infantry of the British right-rear column (the 7th Black Watch) supported by the Shermans of 148th Regiment, Royal Armoured Corps assaults and secures the village of Garcelles-Secqueville.

8. 0445hrs: the 5th Cameron Highlanders, an infantry battalion from 152nd Infantry Brigade, is halted north of the hamlet of Lorguichon by fierce enemy resistance.

9. 0530hrs: with the 2nd Seaforths bogged down in their assault on Tilly-la-Campagne, the 152nd Infantry Brigade's reserve battalion, the 5th Seaforths, is committed to reinforce the attack on Tilly-la-Campagne.

10. 0600hrs: the right-forward British column halts 500m short of its objective – the village of Cramesnil – to regroup and debus its infantry.

11. 0730hrs: the right-forward British column assaults and secures the village of Cramesnil.

12. 0800–0830hrs: with the British right-rear column having completed its capture of Garcelles-Secqueville, a squadron of Shermans from 148th Regiment, Royal Armoured Corps races northwards to attack by surprise the recalcitrant German garrison in Tilly-la-Campagne.

13. 1050hrs: after being overrun by British Sherman tanks, the last remaining 30 German soldiers in Tilly-la-Campagne surrender.

14. 1130hrs: the 5th Black Watch, an infantry battalion from 153rd Infantry Brigade, clears the village of Bourguébus and the farms located further east to secure the left-hand flank of the offensive.

15. 1130hrs: the battered remnants of III Bataillon, Grenadier-Regiment 1055 consolidate new defensive positions in and around La Hogue and Secqueville-la-Campagne.

THE EASTERN (BRITISH) SECTOR OF THE INITIAL TOTALIZE BREAK-IN BATTLE

The British and German dispositions at 2330hrs, 7 August, and the British advance and German resistance through to 1000hrs, 8 August.

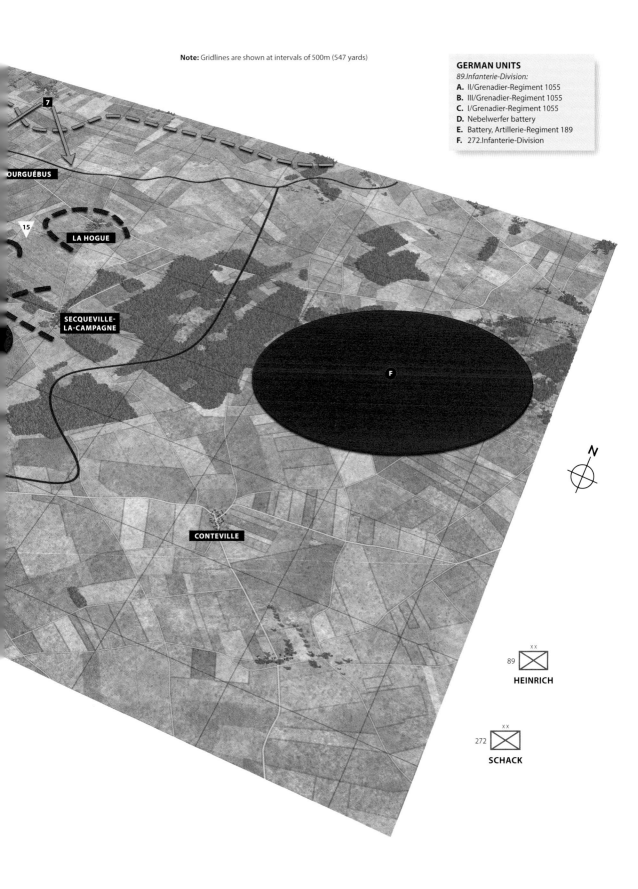

Note: Gridlines are shown at intervals of 500m (547 yards)

GERMAN UNITS
89.Infanterie-Division:
A. II/Grenadier-Regiment 1055
B. III/Grenadier-Regiment 1055
C. I/Grenadier-Regiment 1055
D. Nebelwerfer battery
E. Battery, Artillerie-Regiment 189
F. 272.Infanterie-Division

BOURGUÉBUS

LA HOGUE

SECQUEVILLE-
LA-CAMPAGNE

F

CONTEVILLE

89 HEINRICH

272 SCHACK

machine-gun and small-arms fire into the infiltrators. In this difficult terrain, the Canadians had scant hope of success now that the element of surprise had been lost, and so they hurriedly withdrew north back to the Saint-André-sur-Orne crossroads. The second assault on May-sur-Orne had failed.

Despite these setbacks, Gauvreau realised that his forces had to secure the road through May-sur-Orne so that the Allies could use it to resupply the spearhead mobile columns. Consequently, he decided that Les Fusiliers would have to mount a third attempt to capture the village once daylight emerged, despite the risk of enemy enfilade fire delivered from the high ground located west of the Orne. That morning, as the battalion prepared to mount this third assault, Gauvreau learned that British Churchill Crocodile flame-throwing tanks from the 141st Regiment, RAC were on their way to assist this attack. Gauvreau realised that these terrifying weapons would only help his next attack secure success if his soldiers co-operated effectively with these unfamiliar vehicles. His riflemen would have to prevent Panzerfaust-equipped German soldiers, well hidden in houses, from knocking out the tanks at close range. Yet Les Fusiliers had never undertaken any training in close co-operation with Crocodiles. Undeterred, Gauvreau hastily organised an improvised training session for his men which took place during the middle of the day once the Crocodiles had arrived.

Les Fusiliers' third assault on May-sur-Orne commenced at 1545hrs, 8 August, by which time Totalize Phase II had already begun. Gauvreau committed his entire attenuated battalion – now reduced to just 157 effectives

On 9 August 1944 two infanteers from Les Fusiliers Mont-Royal look down into a mineshaft, part of the sprawling SNCP iron-ore mine complex that stretched between Saint-André-sur-Orne and May-sur-Orne. The Canadians claimed that German troops used these shafts to infiltrate behind the Canadian lines. (Library and Archives Canada PA-131353)

A view showing the utter devastation that Allied liberation inflicted upon the village of May-sur-Orne during the break-in phase of Totalize, 7–8 August 1944. (Library and Archives Canada PA-114504)

– in a two-pronged attack on the village. The western assault force comprised the 60 soldiers of C and D companies plus a troop of Crocodiles, while the 90 riflemen of A and B companies plus two troops of Crocodiles formed the eastern assault force. Both groups advanced across the fields on either side of the north–south road into the village. The Crocodiles fired their 75mm main guns to make holes in the nearby houses' walls, through which they launched their terrifying jets of flame. Then Les Fusiliers kicked down the doors of these burning buildings and, once inside, finished off any surviving defenders with grenades and bayonets. Initially both assault groups encountered bitter enemy resistance, but thereafter the terrified defenders simply fled as the Crocodiles' fearsome jets of flame approached them. By 1800hrs Les Fusiliers had completed the capture of May-sur-Orne and the surrounding area. In retrospect, these events suggest that Simonds' expectation that a successful mobile column assault would enfeeble the German defence of their bypassed forward defended localities had been woefully optimistic.

A section of infanteers from Les Fusiliers Mont-Royal raise a flag after the capture of the village of May-sur-Orne on 9 August 1944. (Library and Archives Canada PA-129143)

The story of the Queen's Own Cameron Highlanders of Canada's attack on Fontenay-le-Marmion also mirrored Les Fusiliers' experiences at May-sur-Orne. Deployed just west of Beauvoir Farm, close to the triple column formation, the Camerons were to march 2,900m south to secure the village of Fontenay-le-Marmion, the most southerly of the four objectives allotted to the marching infantry. The battalion's advance initially progressed well, but the combination of increasing enemy fire and scattered minefields caused a number of delays. Thus it was only at 0500hrs that the Camerons could initiate their assault on the village. By 0630hrs the battalion had secured the northern half of the village. Subsequently the Camerons launched several abortive assaults to secure the southern part of Fontenay-le-Marmion in the face of extremely bitter enemy resistance, during which the Canadians suffered severe casualties. Furthermore, by 0830hrs the tactical situation for the Camerons in Fontenay-le-Marmion had deteriorated. Accurate German artillery and rocket-launcher fire had caused severe casualties within battalion headquarters, hampering the conduct of the battle. Subsequently, the Germans launched several counter-attacks into the Camerons' exposed left (eastern) flank and left rear. These enemy ripostes gained such ground that they actually cut the battalion's lines of communication back to the Allied start line.

In danger of being overrun, the battalion frantically appealed to 2nd Canadian Infantry Division for assistance. Luckily Simonds had held back a proportion of Allied artillery from commitment either to the rolling barrage or counter-battery tasks precisely to deal with requests for emergency defensive fires such as this. In response, Allied artillery poured massed fires down upon the German troops, helping to temporarily stabilise the situation. The 2nd Canadian Infantry Division commander wished to mount a relief

Two soldiers from the Queen's Own Cameron Highlanders of Canada pose for the cameraman with a captured German swastika flag somewhere within the base of Haut Mesnil Quarry during 10 August 1944. (Library and Archives Canada PA-183135)

operation to rescue the Camerons, but his hands were tied by lack of available infantry. As soon as they had cleared Rocquancourt of enemy forces, Foulkes ordered, the Saskatchewans would mount a relief attack towards Fontenay-le-Marmion. Unfortunately, the isolated Camerons had to fend off renewed German attacks until early afternoon, for it took the Saskatchewans until 1330hrs to complete the mopping up of Rocquancourt. Thereafter, two Saskatchewan infantry companies, backed by a Sherman squadron from the 1st Hussars, advanced west from Rocquancourt. This relief force assaulted the German forces at Fontenay-le-Marmion in the flank and rear, while the Camerons simultaneously renewed their frontal attack on the southern half of the village. Between them these forces managed to clear all of Fontenay-le-Marmion by 1535hrs.

The third and final Canadian marching infantry assault, however, proved less problematic than the two assaults just described. Deployed between the triple column formation and the Recce column, the Saskatchewans were to secure the villages of Verrières and Rocquancourt that had been bypassed by the mobile column assault; unlike the other two Canadian marching-infantry assaults, the Saskatchewans hoped to enjoy some benefit from the suppressive effect of the Allied rolling barrage. By marching at the double the infantry managed to keep close to the barrage as it lifted south through Verrières, which they assaulted with some element of surprise. Within an hour the Saskatchewans had captured the village having suffered only modest casualties in the process. Subsequently the infantry advanced south to assault Rocquancourt, through which the Royals' and Hamiltons' columns had previously passed. Here the Saskatchewans became bogged down by intense and dogged German resistance. Only by 1330hrs had the battalion completed the clearance of Rocquancourt, at which point two of its rifle companies rushed south-west to mount the urgent relief operation to assist the beleaguered Camerons that Foulkes had ordered them to commence over three hours previously.

The British infantry assaults

While 6th Canadian Infantry Brigade's three battalions mounted the foot-based assaults on the enemy forward positions bypassed by the four Canadian mobile columns, this pattern was repeated in the British sector located east of the main Caen–Falaise road. Here, two infantry battalions from 152nd Infantry Brigade were to march on foot to secure three locations bypassed by the three British mobile columns. The 5th Camerons were to capture the village of Lorguichon, located south-east of Rocquancourt adjacent to the main road, as well as the nearby woods. Simultaneously, the 2nd Seaforths were to secure the village of Tilly-la-Campagne, located between the axes of advance of the British right and left mobile columns. In addition, elements of 153rd Infantry Brigade were to advance south from Soliers to capture Bourguébus.

The most important of these missions was the capture of Tilly-la-Campagne. The 2nd Seaforths' plan envisaged a three-pronged assault with D Company attacking the village frontally along the iron-ore railway line embankment, while A and B companies respectively mounted left- and right-flanking assaults. At 2350hrs the battalion's three assault companies crossed the start line, while C Company remained in reserve. Subsequently, these three companies silently marched south-east following the Allied rolling barrage as it slowly lifted south-south-east through Tilly-la-Campagne. By 0035hrs, 8 August all three companies had reached their respective start-points for their respective assaults; D Company was deployed on the western side of the embankment, while A and B companies had deployed in the fields located to the east-north-east and west-north-west of Tilly-la-Campagne, respectively.

At 0040hrs the companies began the assault on the village. A Company attacked towards the orchard located north of Tilly-la-Campagne, but by 0110hrs it had been halted by fierce enemy fire, as had B Company's assault. With

An Allied scout car patrols past the wrecked church at May-sur-Orne on 10 August 1944. (Library and Archives Canada PA-169292)

the attack now stalled, the battalion commander, Lieutenant-Colonel George Andrews, committed his reserve, C Company, to restore forward momentum to the A Company assault on the orchard. By 0150hrs, however, C Company's attack had also been pinned down by heavy defensive fire in positions adjacent to those held by C Company. With no reserves left at 0200hrs, Andrews was compelled to request reinforcements from Brigadier James Cassels. In response, at 0213hrs Cassels ordered Captain Murray's D Company, the 5th Seaforth Highlanders to reinforce the faltering attack on Tilly-la-Campagne. Andrews ordered Murray's company to bolster the positions held by B Company west of the village. At 0500hrs Andrews's battalion, augmented by Murray's company, again assaulted Tilly-la-Campagne. Once again, the attacking British forces encountered intense enemy defensive fire, which inflicted a 50 per cent casualty rate on one of Murray's platoons. By 0530hrs it had become clear that the assault on Tilly-la-Campagne had stalled irrevocably.

In the meantime 152nd Infantry Brigade's staff had organised a large artillery bombardment that would accompany what had been planned as a full two-battalion daylight attack on Tilly-la-Campagne mounted by the 2nd and 5th Seaforths. The attack had been slated for 0610hrs but was postponed to 1000hrs due to the emergence of a dense pre-dawn mist. At 0735hrs, as the preparations for the impending set-piece assault continued, Cassels learned that a Sherman squadron from 148th Regiment, RAC had become available after the capture of Garcelles-Secqueville. He requested that the tanks advance 1,600m north-north-west towards Tilly-la-Campagne to strike the defenders from the rear. An hour later, a column of Shermans charged through the dense mist into the village, guns blazing, taking the enemy by

Lieutenant George Galbraith of the Toronto Scottish Regiment, the 2nd Canadian Infantry Division's machine-gun battalion, at Tilly-la-Campagne on 8 August 1944. (Library and Archives Canada PA-132832)

Infantrymen from one of the battalions of the 3rd Canadian Infantry Division advance in dispersed order through the wrecked streets of the hamlet of Lorguichon, located just within the British sector, on 9 August 1944. (Library and Archives Canada PA-129137)

surprise. Over the ensuing hour the tanks devastated the German positions in and around Tilly-la-Campagne, prompting the enemy to parley concerning a capitulation before the set-piece infantry assault had even begun. At 1055hrs 32 enemy soldiers surrendered and over the ensuing 30 minutes a further 19 prisoners were taken; Tilly-la-Campagne had finally been captured.

While the Seaforths fought this bitter struggle to secure Tilly-la-Campagne, some 900m further west, close to the main Caen–Falaise road, the 5th Camerons mounted their own foot-based operation. From their start line near La Guinguette, just east of the assembly area of the two British right columns, the Camerons were to advance 3,400m south-south-east to capture both the hamlet of Lorguichon and Lorguichon Woods to the south-east. At 2355hrs, after the delay caused by the late departure of the right-rear column, the 5th Camerons eventually began marching south-south-east across the fields of La Chasse in the wake of the two right columns. Initially marching to the east of these mobile columns' axes of advance, the 5th Camerons soon veered to the right, heading due south to cross over onto the western side of the mobile columns' axes of advance. With the barrage gradually receding into the distance beyond them, the 5th Camerons then marched parallel with the main road in the face of light German defensive fire.

Subsequently, as the battalion's infantrymen marched across the cornfields of Le Laumel, they were repeatedly held up by the fire of well-concealed enemy snipers who inflicted a number of casualties. Clearing the area of enemy forces yielded 34 prisoners but took the battalion 50 minutes. Thus it was only at 0330hrs that the battalion reached the northern fringes of its objective, Lorguichon. While two rifle companies of the 5th Camerons launched a double-pronged frontal assault on Lorguichon, a third made a left-flanking move to assault the nearby Lorguichon Woods. By 0445hrs the 5th Camerons had completed the clearance of both Lorguichon and the adjacent woods. Subsequently, the battalion's soldiers frantically dug defensive positions and carefully sited their Bren guns and PIAT launchers, ready to repel the likely immediate enemy local counter-attack. Just as with the Canadian sector, some of the British marching infantry assaults on the enemy forward positions bypassed by the column assault had proven significantly more challenging than Allied planning had imagined. This reality attested to the defensive potency of many of the German forward defended localities.

Phase I's achievements
Faced with a powerful German defensive system that was augmented by the terrain, Simonds had taken a considerable gamble in ordering a bi-divisional night assault employing novel infiltration tactics executed by mobile columns. Securing surprise in timing and

method, the gamble paid off. By midday on 8 August, the Allied attacks mounted during Totalize Phase I had secured impressive success. The human price of this success – II Canadian Corps suffered 385 battle casualties – compared extremely favourably with previous Allied break-in offensives mounted during the Normandy campaign. Five of the seven Allied spearhead mobile columns had secured their objectives, while the remaining two had also secured significant territorial advances. Two of the five marching infantry attacks, moreover, had secured their objectives and the remaining three would subsequently complete their missions that afternoon.

This innovative Allied surprise night-time infiltration break-in offensive had secured stunning territorial advances, certainly in comparison with the other Allied offensives previously mounted in Normandy. In the space of just 13 hours Simonds' forces had advanced up to 6,000m deep right through the initial German defensive position across a 7,200m frontage. While further consolidation and mopping-up was required, by 1230hrs, 8 August, Totalize Phase I had effectively destroyed the initial enemy defensive position. Could Simonds' forces exploit this remarkable success during the offensive's second phase?

TOTALIZE PHASE II COMMENCES

During the late morning of 8 August, Simonds' Phase II spearheads – the 4th Canadian and Polish 1st Armoured divisions – moved south to their slated jumping-off positions that ran from Pièce-de-Caillouet in the west through to Saint-Aignan-de-Cramesnil in the east. Meanwhile, some 681 USAAF B-17 Flying Fortress heavy day bombers approached the Normandy coast; their mission was to support Totalize Phase II – the daytime break-in operation directed against the enemy's Bretteville–Saint-Sylvain defence line. As the lead Pathfinder aircraft reached the Falaise plain, they identified the aim points for the following bombers by dropping flares onto these six targets while simultaneously Allied artillery fired red smoke rounds onto them. Subsequently, between 1226 and 1355hrs some 497 B-17s successfully delivered 1,487 tons of high explosive onto their targets. The remaining 184

Sergeant Ben Landriault from the Toronto Scottish Regiment's carrier platoon smoking a cigarette during a lull in the action in the village of Tilly-la-Campagne on 8 August 1944. (Library and Archives Canada PA-141857)

bombers, however, had to abort their runs, some of them having been driven off course by the intense anti-aircraft fire put up by the III Flakkorps. The remaining aircraft – having failed to identify their targets with certainty due to the combination of thick dust, rising smoke and patchy ground mist – aborted their missions rather than risk friendly fire casualties. However, some such incidents still occurred, in which at least 65 Canadian and Polish troops were killed, plus another 260 wounded.

The German riposte
As Simonds' forces regrouped during the late morning awaiting the second bombing strike, local German commanders strove to organise a classic doctrinal local counter-attack. Around 1145hrs, General Hans Eberbach, 5.Panzerarmee commander, came forward to Cintheaux to discuss the critical situation with SS-

Oberführer Kurt Meyer, the commander of the 'Hitlerjugend' division. Next, Meyer and SS-Sturmbannführer Hans Waldmüller drove 1,100m north to the gentle rise situated north-east of Gaumesnil where they undertook a personal reconnaissance of the situation. The innovative Allied night-time attack had caught I SS-Panzerkorps by surprise, and the mobile column assault had penetrated much of the German initial position, with only limited forces managing to withdraw south in good order. The second German defensive line, located 3,000m south of the current front, was still manned merely by scratch forces and thus remained vulnerable to a renewed Allied armoured onslaught.

By the time that Meyer had completed this reconnaissance at 1155hrs he had decided that his forces had to initiate an immediate spoiling counter-attack to at least delay (and at best prevent) the Allied armour from attacking south to break through the second German line. Meyer hoped that his forces, despite being outnumbered, might achieve sufficient surprise to stall the impending start of Totalize Phase II. At noon Meyer ordered the available elements of Kampfgruppe Waldmüller to attack north towards Saint-Aignan-de-Cramesnil at 1230hrs on an axis just east of the main Caen–Falaise road. This force comprised 500 Panzergrenadiers, ten tank destroyers, 20 Panzer IVs and Vs, and four Tiger tanks from SS-Hauptsturmführer Michael Wittmann's 2nd Company, schwere SS-Panzer-Abteilung 101. The riposte faced daunting odds, however, for no fewer than eight Allied armoured regiments or infantry battalions were then deployed in the La Jalousie–Saint-Aignan-de-Cramesnil sector.

Next, at 1210hrs, while Meyer and Waldmüller were briefing Wittmann at Cintheaux, the officers observed a solitary Allied bomber aircraft dropping coloured flares. They deduced that this must be an Allied pathfinder aircraft identifying the aiming points for a heavy bombing strike that was in all probably just a few minutes away from being initiated. Realising that he now had little choice, Meyer ordered his subordinates to launch their attacks immediately. From experience he knew that the Allies usually left a safety zone between their own ground forces and the bombers' aim

An extremely rare colour photograph of Totalize. An Allied vehicle, described as being hit by a German mortar bomb, burns furiously near Cintheaux, streaming acrid smoke into the otherwise clear summer skies during the late afternoon of 8 August. (Library and Archives Canada PA-e010786219)

The second Totalize break-in battle, 1200–2359hrs, 8 August 1944.

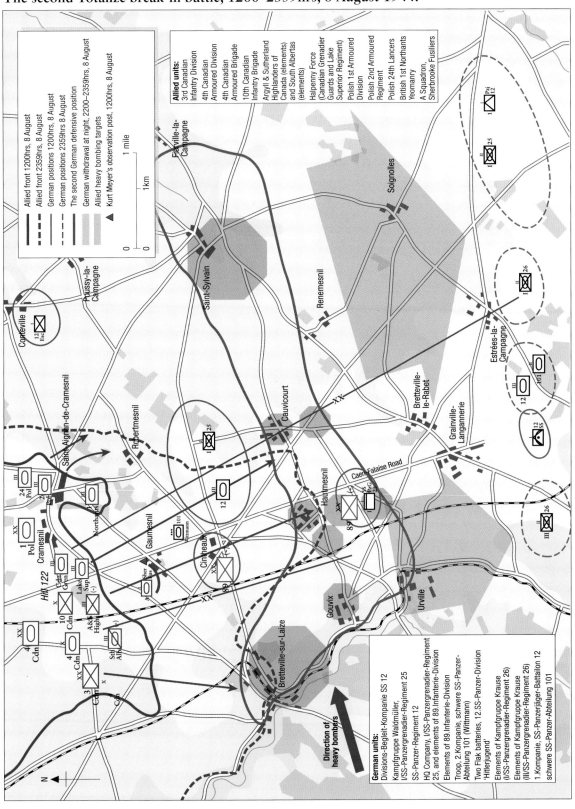

Legend:
- Allied front 1200hrs, 8 August
- Allied front 2359hrs, 8 August
- German positions 1200hrs, 8 August
- German positions 2359hrs 8 August
- The second German defensive position
- German withdrawal at night, 2200–2359hrs, 8 August
- Allied heavy bombing targets
- Kurt Meyer's observation post, 1200hrs, 8 August

1 mile
1km

Allied units:
3rd Canadian Infantry Division
4th Canadian Armoured Division
4th Canadian Armoured Brigade
10th Canadian Infantry Brigade
Argyll & Sutherland Highlanders of Canada (elements) and South Albertas (elements)
Halpenny Force (Canadian Grenadier Guards and Lake Superior Regiment)
Polish 1st Armoured Division
Polish 2nd Armoured Regiment
Polish 24th Lancers
British 1st Northants Yeomanry
A Squadron, Sherbrooke Fusiliers

German units:
Divisions-Begleit-Kompanie SS 12
Kampfgruppe Waldmüller, I/SS-Panzergrenadier-Regiment 25
SS-Panzer-Regiment 12
HQ Company, I/SS-Panzergrenadier-Regiment 25, and elements of 89.Infanterie-Division
Elements of 89.Infanterie-Division
Troop, 2.Kompanie, schwere SS-Panzer-Abteilung 101 (Wittmann)
Two Flak batteries, 12.SS-Panzer-Division 'Hitlerjugend'
Elements of Kampfgruppe Krause (I/SS-Panzergrenadier-Regiment 26)
Elements of Kampfgruppe Krause (III/SS-Panzergrenadier-Regiment 26)
1.Kompanie, SS-Panzerjäger-Battalion 12
schwere SS-Panzer-Abteilung 101

Direction of heavy bombers

Caen–Falaise Road

An open-backed Allied lorry apparently carrying jerrycans moves forward along a dusty road towards the flaming wreck of an Allied vehicle that had allegedly been hit by enemy 88mm gunfire. (Library and Archives Canada PA-169288)

View from inside Le Petit Ravin a 900m-long and 15m-deep U-shaped defile that was not even indicated on Allied maps. The German's intimate knowledge of the battlefield provided them with evident tactical advantages. The trees inside the defile are a post-war feature. (Author's collection)

points; if the German forces counter-attacked the current Allied front, they would enter this zone and thus evade the devastation inflicted by the heavy bombers.

Around 1225hrs the leading tanks and dismounted Panzergrenadiers that formed the eastern element of Kampfgruppe Waldmüller began to move north from the Les Jardinets–Les Ruelles area. The tanks rumbled north, halting in the occasional shallow depressions encountered to fire on suspected Allied positions on Hill 122, Cramesnil and Saint-Aignan-de-Cramesnil, while the Panzergrenadiers scurried north trying to keep up as best they could. Unbeknown to the Germans, elements of a British Sherman tank regiment – the 1st Northamptonshire Yeomanry (1st Northants) – had recently moved forward from Saint-Aignan-de-Cramesnil to occupy the orchards located south-west of the latter village at Delle-de-la-Rocque. Meanwhile, on the western flank of the attack, Wittmann's troop of four Tiger tanks also steadily rumbled north-north-east on an axis just 150m east of the main road. Within minutes of spotting this mass of Panzers advancing towards them, the Allied units deployed in the area had called down accurate artillery defensive fire onto them. Although this fire failed to cause significant vehicular losses, it soon forced most of the Panzergrenadiers accompanying the tanks to go to ground.

By 1255hrs the Panzers and their accompanying infantry on the right flank had successfully pushed north to reach the various thick tree-hedges located north of Daumesnil. Using these as cover from Allied observation and fire, the German forces continued to work their way stealthily north-north-east to reach the southern entrances to Le Petit Ravin – a peculiar U-shaped defile situated 770m south of Saint-Aignan-de-Cramesnil. Waldmüller's tanks then infiltrated 900m south-west through the defile to engage the 1st Northants from the eastern flank. During the next 45 minutes a bitter and confused series of engagements raged in and around the western end of the defile. Eventually intense Allied tank, anti-tank, artillery, PIAT and small-arms fire forced the German forces to withdraw in some confusion. The ferocity of this action was indicated by the 20 destroyed or damaged Sherman tanks and the 11 knocked out or abandoned Panzers that now littered the area around the defile.

While the savage battle for the defile raged, the situation remained quiet for the western elements of the 1st Northants, deployed in the Delle orchards. One such element was No. 3 Troop from A Squadron. Its four Sherman tanks included Sergeant Gordon's Firefly, whose gunner was Trooper Joe Ekins. At around 1235hrs the British spotted a group of three Tigers heading north-north-east adjacent to the main Caen–Falaise road; unbeknown to them they had spotted Wittmann's troop. The Tigers were advancing in line-ahead formation, suggesting that their crews did not yet know that the Yeomanry had recently occupied the Delle orchards, as the tanks' less invulnerable flanks were exposed. Believing that they had not been detected, the British calmly waited until the Tigers had closed to within 800m range. Between 1240 and 1252hrs, according to the 1st Northants war diary, Ekins fired five rounds and scored hits on three Tigers. That said, during this period Canadian Fireflies of the Sherbrooke Fusiliers were also engaging the Tigers from their positions located at Gaumesnil, west of the main road, at a range of 1,100m. Similarly, British 144th Regiment, RAC Fireflies, located on Hill 122, were engaging the Tigers at a range of 1,300m. Somewhere amid this deluge of tank fire all four Tigers were knocked out, Wittmann's tank exploding, blowing off the turret and killing the SS-Panzer ace and his entire crew. Thus the western element of Waldmüller's counter-attack force suffered the same fate as the eastern elements – resoundingly defeated with heavy losses. But at least Meyer could console himself with the thought that, despite the defeat of his riposte with the grievous loss of 16 precious tanks, his forces had bought some additional time by seemingly delaying the commencement of Totalize Phase II.

The Canadian advance

At 1355hrs on 8 August Simonds' two spearhead armoured divisions commenced Totalize Phase II, the daytime assault on the German reserve defensive line. The offensive resumed at exactly the intended time. The long pause during the late morning after the completion of the initial break-in battle had been planned to allow time for the heavy bombing strikes to be executed. Thus it was entirely coincidental that the offensive resumed immediately after Waldmüller's riposte had been repelled; the sacrifice of 16 precious Panzers had neither bought the Germans any extra time to build-up their defensive strength along the second position nor had it exerted any significant spoiling effect on the resumed Totalize offensive.

A heavily camouflaged Sherman Firefly. Although this tank had the same vulnerabilities to enemy fire as an ordinary Sherman, its potent 17pdr gun did allow it to compete more than favourably in lethality with even the deadly German Tiger I heavy tank. (Library and Archives Canada PA-130935)

The resumed offensive was spearheaded by the 4th Canadian Armoured Division, deployed across the western sector, and the Polish 1st Armoured Division, deployed to the east. The dividing line between the divisions was just to the east of the main Caen–Falaise road. Both divisions possessed very narrow attack frontages – a decision made by Simonds that both divisional commanders queried on the grounds that it constricted their freedom for tactical manoeuvre. Although not an experienced armoured commander himself, the forceful corps commander, however, refused to change this aspect of the corps plan. That afternoon both divisions struck south in their first experiences of combat as a coherent formation, although

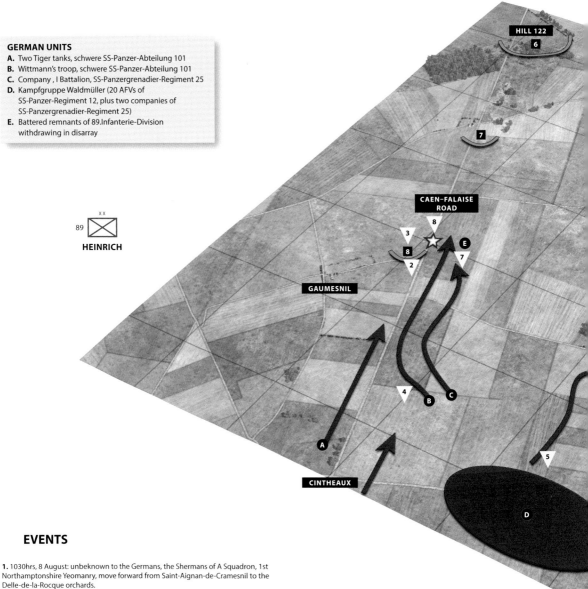

GERMAN UNITS
A. Two Tiger tanks, schwere SS-Panzer-Abteilung 101
B. Wittmann's troop, schwere SS-Panzer-Abteilung 101
C. Company , I Battalion, SS-Panzergrenadier-Regiment 25
D. Kampfgruppe Waldmüller (20 AFVs of
SS-Panzer-Regiment 12, plus two companies of
SS-Panzergrenadier-Regiment 25)
E. Battered remnants of 89.Infanterie-Division
withdrawing in disarray

89   HEINRICH

HILL 122
6

CAEN–FALAISE ROAD

GAUMESNIL

CINTHEAUX

EVENTS

1. 1030hrs, 8 August: unbeknown to the Germans, the Shermans of A Squadron, 1st Northamptonshire Yeomanry, move forward from Saint-Aignan-de-Cramesnil to the Delle-de-la-Rocque orchards.

2. 1145–1200hrs: Kurt Meyer and Hans Waldmüller go forward to conduct a personal reconnaissance in the vicinity of Gaumesnil.

3. 1205–1225hrs: elements of A Squadron, Sherbrooke Fusiliers, move forward to Gaumesnil.

4. 1220hrs: Michael Wittmann in Tiger 007 leads a troop of four Tiger tanks in an advance north-north-west just to the east of the main Caen–Falaise road, accompanied by a company from I Bataillon, SS-Panzergrenadier-Regiment 25.

5. 1255hrs: elements of Kampfgruppe Waldmüller begin to advance north towards Le Petit Ravin, an unusual U-shaped defile that runs west to east just to the south of Saint-Aignan-de-Cramesnil. The Kampfgruppe, formed from elements of 12.SS-Panzer-Division 'Hitlerjugend' consists of around 20 Panzer IVs and Panthers from SS-Panzer-Regiment 12 plus two companies from SS-Panzergrenadier-Regiment 25.

6. 1300–1310hrs: the tanks of Kampfgruppe Waldmüller use the lateral tree-hedge lines located around the Robertmesnil farm complex to conceal their advance towards Le Petit Ravin.

7. 1235–1245hrs: Wittmann's troop of Tigers receives accurate Allied artillery and anti-tank fire. The latter is delivered by the elements of the 1st Northamptonshire Yeomanry deployed in the Delle-de-la-Rocque orchards, the Canadian Sherbrooke Fusiliers in the Gaumesnil–Hill 122 area and the 144th Regiment, Royal Armoured Corps around Gaumesnil.

8. 1240–1250hrs: Michael Wittmann's Tiger is destroyed by Allied tank fire, as well as at least two more of the accompanying Tigers. The western German riposte now stalls.

9. 1315–1345hrs: the AFVs of Kampfgruppe Waldmüller reach and enter Le Petit Ravin, where a bitter close-range tank battle ensues with the 1st Northamptonshire Yeomanry.

10. 1345–1355hrs: the few surviving German tanks withdraw south from Le Petit Ravin. This encounter has left 16 knocked-out German tanks and 13 Allied ones littering the battlefield.

THE GERMAN COUNTER-ATTACK AROUND SAINT-AIGNAN-DE-CRAMESNIL

The Allied and German dispositions around noon on 8 August and the German counter-attacks, 1220–1355hrs.

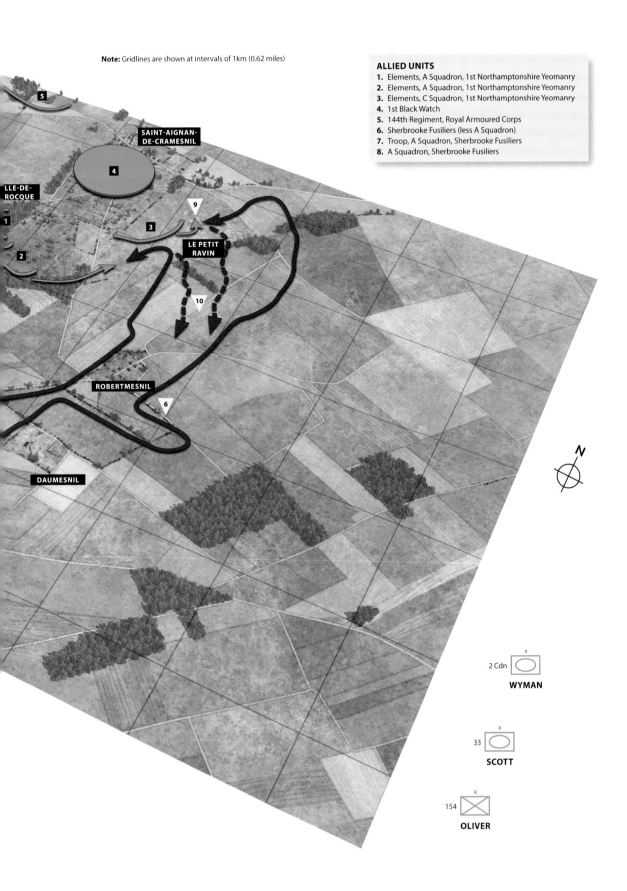

Note: Gridlines are shown at intervals of 1km (0.62 miles)

SAINT-AIGNAN-
DE-CRAMESNIL

LLE-DE-
ROCQUE

LE PETIT
RAVIN

ROBERTMESNIL

DAUMESNIL

N

2 Cdn
WYMAN

33
SCOTT

154
OLIVER

significant elements in the Polish division possessed considerable prior unit-level combat experience. The dividing line between the two divisional sectors started 780m east of the main Caen–Falaise road south of Hill 122 and ran south-south-east roughly parallel to the main road past the church located south-west of Cauvicourt.

The 4th Canadian Armoured Division commander, Major-General George Kitching, in turn divided his divisional sector into two even narrower brigade-level sub-sectors, a mere 780m wide; the main road was the dividing line between these brigade fronts. To the east of the main road was the front held by the 4th Canadian Armoured Brigade, while to the west was the 10th Canadian Infantry Brigade front. The 4th Canadian Armoured Brigade attack was spearheaded by the newly formed Halpenny Force battle group. At 1355hrs Halpenny Force began to advance south heading for the gap between the hamlets of Gaumesnil and Robertmesnil. Lieutenant-Colonel Bill Halpenny's task force comprised a Sherman regiment, the Canadian Grenadier Guards, together with a motor battalion, the Lake Superior Regiment, to form a mixed armoured and mobile infantry battle group.

In its first combat Halpenny Force advanced cautiously, however, partly because it experienced communication problems that prevented effective employment of on-call artillery fire support but also because its left (eastern) flank remained wide open. All of 4th Canadian Armoured Division's units, moreover, were fully aware of the long-range lethality of German tank and anti-tank weapons in such open terrain. Soon exhortations to develop greater forward momentum came down to Halpenny Force from division and brigade. The divisional commander, then located at his tactical HQ near La Jalousie, repeatedly urged 4th Canadian Armoured Brigade HQ to instil greater forward offensive momentum in its spearheads. When the 4th Canadian Armoured Brigade commander Brigadier Leslie Booth failed to respond to divisional messages, Kitching went forward to the brigade's tactical HQ to investigate. Here Kitching found Booth in a drunken stupor in his command tank! After berating Booth for dereliction of duty, Kitching ordered him to instil greater momentum to his units' advance. Astonishingly Kitching did not immediately relieve Booth of command, perhaps because there was no obvious suitable replacement; sadly, Booth was killed just six days later.

By 1820hrs, a by now badly dispersed Halpenny Force had been halted by enemy fire some 1,000m north of the village of Bretteville-le-Rabet after a 3,900m advance. This prompted Kitching to commit to battle his only available divisional reserve, the 12th Manitoba Dragoons, normally II Canadian Corps' armoured car regiment. Kitching ordered the 12th Manitobas to race 7,100m south from Rocquancourt to Halpenny Force's position, where it was to mount a right-flanking assault on Bretteville-le-Rabet. As the 12th Manitobas tried to advance

Universal carriers of the Toronto Scottish Regiment move forward across open ground interspersed with a few trees during 8 August 1944. (Library and Archives Canada PA-166807)

The 12th Manitoba Dragoons were II Canadian Corps' allocated armoured car regiment, intended for recce tasks. The Manitobas employed Staghound T17E1 armoured cars such as these, seen here crossing the Seine River in late August 1944. (Library and Archives Canada PA-144143)

south, they became bogged down in traffic congestion around the main road, which meant that their slated attack could not be launched before dark set in. Next, at 1900hrs, after hearing that Halpenny Force had been driven onto the defence north of Bretteville-le-Rabet, Kitching ordered the battle group to mount a hasty evening assault on the village before darkness arrived. It proved impossible to form up for this attack before darkness set in, so the Halpenny Force commander postponed the assault until dawn and followed doctrine by withdrawing his tanks to a night harbour at Cintheaux. During the afternoon of 8 August, 4th Canadian Armoured Brigade had not even managed to secure its initial objective, the clearing of Bretteville-le-Rabet, let alone achieve the 12,800m advance to hills 195 and 206 anticipated by Simonds.

West of the main Caen–Falaise road, meanwhile, the 10th Canadian Infantry Brigade assault also unfolded. After initial delays caused by severe traffic congestion, at 1600hrs a task force of eight South Alberta Regiment Sherman tanks, plus two infantry companies from the 1st Battalion, Argyll and Sutherland Highlanders (Princess Louise's) mounted a methodical set-piece attack on Cintheaux backed by heavy artillery fire support. The assault secured success in the face of very light enemy opposition in what was probably just a platoon outpost. This revealed the degree of caution and reliance on set-piece attacks evident in the 'green' 4th Canadian Armoured Division; for having just arrived in theatre the formation had had no opportunity to acclimatise to the realities of combat in Normandy.

By 1730hrs, the South Albertas–1st Argyll and Sutherlands battle group had successfully advanced 1,200m south on an

A Canadian half-track moves through the village of Cintheaux during the late afternoon of 8 August 1944 during Phase II of Operation Totalize. (Library and Archives Canada PA-129138)

A view of the wide expanse of Haut Mesnil Quarry taken on 10 August 1944, a day after its capture. The Germans had used the site as a depot and munitions store. (Library and Archives Canada PA-169294)

axis 230m west of the main road to assault the village of Haut Mesnil and beyond it the extensive and deep Haut Mesnil Quarry, which restricted the opportunities that existed for the Canadians to conduct tactical manoeuvre. By 1900hrs, the Canadian force had secured Haut Mesnil after a fierce battle. However, during the next two hours the battle group struggled to push further south towards the quarry due to the bitter resistance offered by the scratch Sperrgruppe Klein. This ad-hoc grouping had been formed around the headquarters of I Bataillon, SS-Panzergrenadier-Regiment 25, when the battalion's staff company had forcibly intercepted disorganised 89.Infanterie-Division stragglers, then streaming south in disarray, and reorganised them into a scratch defensive unit. Finally, one Sherman troop tried to outflank Klein's position, but was knocked out by long-range enemy anti-tank fire from the 8.8cm flak guns Kurt Meyer had just redeployed north of Potigny to dominate the main road. As night descended, the 1st Argyll and Sutherlands abandoned their assault while the surviving Shermans withdrew north to Cintheaux to harbour for the night. Like 4th Canadian Armoured Brigade, 10th Canadian Infantry Brigade had not even managed to secure its initial objectives. The start of Totalize Phase II had been a real disappointment for Kitching, with an advance of just 4,400m instead of the 13,000m envisaged by Simonds. The corps commander reacted to this failure to achieve his aspirations with growing frustration that turned into fury. This anger prompted decisions that would have grave consequences for the future development of Totalize.

The Poles advance

As the 4th Canadian Armoured Division operation unfolded at the start of Totalize Phase II, away to the east the Polish 1st Armoured Division assault also began from 1355hrs. While the Polish division had never fought as a complete formation before, was brand new to the theatre and was hampered by linguistic challenges when interfacing with II Canadian Corps, it did contain numerous veteran sub-units and deployed many senior officers who possessed considerable combat experience that stretched as far back as World War I. The highly experienced divisional commander, Major-General Stanisław Maczek, entrusted the initial assault to his veteran 10th Armoured Cavalry Brigade, which he had personally commanded in the rank of colonel during the 1939 German invasion of Poland.

The 10th Armoured Cavalry Brigade commander in turn decided, despite the narrow frontage imposed by Simonds, to start the assault 'two up', employing the Polish 2nd Armoured Regiment and the 24th Lancers. At 1355hrs both armoured regiments struck south and south-east from the area immediately north-east of Saint-Aignan-de-Cramesnil. The two units formed up in dense formation with two squadrons forward and one in reserve. The division had on-call fire support from its own organic artillery and an Army Group, Royal Artillery, although this had been severely disrupted due to the casualties caused by the friendly fire short-bombing incidents. Simonds had anticipated that the heavy bombing of the enemy reserve positions in the area to the immediate south between Cauvicourt and Saint-Sylvain would suppress the enemy to the south of the 10th Armoured Cavalry Brigade front, and that the initial Phase II assault would thus prove relatively straightforward.

Unfortunately, it was not to be. With scant intelligence on the enemy situation available to them, the Poles enjoyed little situational awareness. During the planning they had been concerned about their completely open left (eastern) flank, against which unknown enemy forces yet untouched by the unfolding Totalize offensive posed a serious threat to their advance. To make matters worse, in the wake of his abortive counter-strike, Waldmüller's remaining tanks had concealed themselves behind the many small copses, tree lines and thick hedges found across the area south of Daumesnil and Robertmesnil, in areas untouched by the recent bombing strikes. Backed by heavy mortar and artillery fires, these dispositions created an effective German killing zone. It was into this zone that the Polish tanks now unwittingly advanced. Between 1435 and 1455hrs, and without the benefit of suppressive artillery fires, the Polish tanks pushed south-east across the eastern fringes of Le Petit Ravin defile. As they did so they encountered a deluge of accurate German tank, anti-tank and artillery fire. A terrifying

Seemingly in noticeably high spirits, personnel from the Polish 1st Armoured Division pose for this photograph around a jeep somewhere in France, 7 August 1944. The slogan written on the vehicle's front reads 'On to Warsaw' via 'Normandy and Berlin'; this phrase perhaps reveals much about Polish troops' real aspirations. (Library and Archives Canada PA-074094)

Soldiers of the Polish 1st Armoured Division gather around the grave of a Canadian soldier to pay their respects, near Caen, on the hot and sunny day of 7 August 1944. (Library and Archives Canada PA-114061)

Soldiers of the Polish 1st Armoured Division talk, probably in basic French, with a female French civilian and her child, who have been pushing carts with apparently whatever could be salvaged from their presumably now destroyed house, August 1944. (Library and Archives Canada PA-129202)

baptism of fire now ensued as Sherman after Sherman exploded after being hit by German rounds. Despite mounting losses, the Polish squadrons bravely pushed on, but after yet more tanks were hit and exploded, the brigade commander issued the order to withdraw back to the original start lines. Once there the survivors looked back and to their horror could observe no fewer than 38 wrecked Polish tanks spewing smoke into the clear summer skies. One can hardly imagine a more shocking introduction to the realities of warfare in Normandy – that in open terrain such as this the unsuppressed enemy possessed tremendous long-range killing-power.

Around 1600hrs, after some hurried reorganisation and repair to the more lightly damaged Shermans, the spearhead squadrons of the Polish 1st Armoured Division courageously resumed their assault south from the Saint-Aignan-de-Cramesnil area. With the backing of artillery concentrations, the Polish armoured columns pushed forward across the battlespace still littered with burning Allied tanks. In the face of heavy German defensive fires, the squadrons managed by dusk to push forward some 1,600m. By nightfall the division's vanguard elements had closed up on the lateral road that ran westward from Cintheaux to Saint-Sylvain. This accomplishment was a reasonable one given the nature of the tactical challenge – an armoured advance across open terrain with minimal artillery fire support against a powerful grouping of German long-range fires that had not been suppressed by the aerial bombing. That said, the Polish advance was far short of the decisive charge south that Simonds had anticipated in his corps plan, and the increasingly frustrated corps commander was in no mood to hear any explanations, however valid, of why this had not been achieved.

The odyssey of Worthington Force

The unfolding failure of Simonds' two armoured divisions to achieve decisive advances southward during the afternoon of 8 August caused the corps commander to grow ever more angry. While Simonds was not experienced in commanding armour, his neat engineer's mind believed strongly that in the wake of the suppressive effect provided by the strategic bombing attacks, his two spearhead armoured divisions ought to have swiftly broken through the second German defensive line and then raced south to secure the hills north of Falaise by nightfall. Irrespective of the feasibility of this scheme, Simonds rightly recognised that in stymieing his armour's attack that afternoon, the meagre forces the enemy currently deployed against II Canadian Corps had managed to secure a significant German tactical success.

This setback could not be allowed to stand, and so Simonds issued new orders at 2100hrs. Throwing existing Allied doctrine into the dustbin, Simonds ordered an astonished Kitching to continue his 4th Canadian Armoured Division assault relentlessly throughout the night. In effect, this was an impromptu repetition of the successful, well-planned Phase I night break-in assault. Kitching's mission was to secure the original objectives set for Phase II – the capture of the crucial high ground of Hill 195, north of Fontaine-le-Pin; from this vantage point the Allies could observe the western exits of Falaise, located 10,000m further south. In his subsequent Orders Group, Kitching ordered Brigadier Booth's 4th Canadian Armoured Brigade to advance 1,800m to secure the village of Bretteville-le-Rabet. At the same time 4th Canadian Armoured Brigade was also to advance 7,600m to secure Hill 195. Booth ordered the existing Halpenny Force battle group to capture Bretteville-le-Rabet. For the execution of the much more daunting and risky night infiltration to Hill 195, Booth ordered the creation of a new all-arms grouping named Worthington Force battle group.

During the very night that these daring assaults were launched, 8–9 August, the Germans – according to their normal practice in Normandy – took advantage of the lull in the devastating Allied fighter-bomber and accurate artillery strikes to redeploy and resupply their forces. Under the cover of darkness the enemy employed tracked, wheeled and horse-drawn vehicles, plus hundreds of bicycles, to bring forward desperately needed ammunition and rations. The German defence now relied heavily on Meyer's 'Hitlerjugend' division, together with the badly weakened – yet surprisingly still cohesive – remnants of 89.Infanterie-Division.

To the west of the main road, part of Kampfgruppe Krause (comprising III Bataillon, SS-Panzergrenadier-Regiment 26) withdrew and established new defensive positions on the key terrain of Hill 195, which was Worthington Force's objective. Simultaneously, east of the road the rest of Kampfgruppe Krause (formed around I Bataillon, SS-Panzergrenadier-Regiment 26) withdrew and established a new defensive line that ran north-east from the ridge by the Mines de Soumont to Point 134, located 800m north of Ouilly-le-Tesson. Meanwhile, Kampfgruppe Waldmüller (now formed from I Bataillon, SS-Panzergrenadier-Regiment 25 and 1.Kompanie, SS-Panzerjäger-Abteilung 12) established a new defensive line that ran east-north-east from Point 134 across the southern slopes of the Hill 140 ridge feature to the hills north-west of Maizières. Meyer's remaining 24 Panzer IV and Panther tanks, together with the eight operational Tigers of schwere SS-Panzer-Abteilung 101, concentrated in Quesnay Wood, where they could be hidden from the scourge of Allied tactical air power. The Quesnay Wood position, which lay north of the new enemy-defended line, dominated any attempted Allied advance down the main Caen–Falaise road.

Simultaneously, German artillery units withdrew to new positions south of Le Laison River, particularly around Saint-Quentin and Montboint. The 'Hitlerjugend' division headquarters remained at Château Le Mont Joly. Nearby the division had established two well-chosen observation posts (OPs) on the high ground through which the Laison Gorge cut: the *Tombeau de Marie Joly* shrine on the gorge's eastern edge, and the rocky outcrop of La Brèche au Diable on its western shoulder. Both OPs provided excellent observation to the north, covering the Hill 140 ridge feature; once again, here the Germans ably exploited their intimate knowledge of the ground to augment their defensive endeavours.

At 0005hrs, 9 August, 4th Canadian Armoured Brigade ordered Worthington Force to commence its night-time mission. This task force comprised the Sherman tanks of the British Columbia Regiment, two

Personnel of the Headquarters Squadron, the British Columbia Regiment, part of the ill-fated Worthington Force, are seen here chatting by their well-camouflaged Sherman tank, later on in the North-West Europe campaign. (Library and Archives Canada PA-151370)

embussed infantry companies from the Algonquin Regiment and other supporting arms. Lieutenant-Colonel Donald Worthington, the British Columbias' commander, led the task force, which was named after him. Its mission was to mount an audacious 7,600m night-time infiltration advance south-south-west to seize Hill 195, the vital high ground north of Fontaine-le-Pin. The battle group was to secure this objective by dawn, so that it could establish strong defensive positions before the predictable daytime German counter-attacks began. A series of difficulties, however, delayed the assembly of Worthington Force's constituent elements. Thus it was not until 0400hrs, 9 August, that the force was ready to set off from its start line near the hamlet of Gaumesnil, close to where Wittmann's Tiger had been destroyed the previous day. Thus Worthington Force now had little more than two hours of the protective shroud of darkness in which to cover the 7,600m to Hill 195.

Having set off at 0402hrs from Gaumesnil, Worthington Force's vehicular columns headed south down the main Caen–Falaise road. When the battle group reached the Haut Mesnil area, however, it became entangled with vehicular columns from Halpenny Force, which had encountered fierce enemy resistance during its assault on Bretteville-le-Rabet. To disentangle his columns from Halpenny's forces, Worthington decided to divert his advance south-east along an ancient, raised grass track, the Chemin Haussé du Duc Guillaume. Having moved 2,000 yards south-east along this track, Worthington then intended to head south-west to rejoin the main Caen–Falaise road south of Grainville and from there continue the advance to Hill 195 as planned.

Abandoned German vehicles, equipment and clothing can be seen here within the flat interior of Haut Mesnil Quarry on 11 August 1944; note the light field railway track in the foreground. (Library and Archives Canada PA-115525)

Between 0420 and 0530hrs, Worthington Force advanced at good speed, trying to make up for lost time, in the face of sporadic enemy defensive fires that seemed to have been delivered from every conceivable point on the compass. During the inevitable chaos of such an advance, many vehicles dropped away from the column and the lead navigators became horribly disorientated and lost. With hindsight it is clear that the column inadvertently continued to advance south-east along the Chemin Haussé rather than turning back south-west to return to the main Caen–Falaise road, although this was not realised by Worthington Force's commanders.

As the first glimmers of pre-dawn emerged Worthington Force's senior commanders had become agitated by the realisation that they were horribly lost. Thankfully, at around 0535hrs the lead vehicles sighted in the distance some high ground. Mightily relieved, the commanders concluded, perhaps rather optimistically, that this high ground must be their objective, Hill 195. Worthington Force now raced unwittingly south-east along the Chemin Haussé towards the high ground to secure it before dawn arrived and exposed them to enemy observation. At 0655hrs Worthington Force reported to 4th Canadian Armoured Brigade that what remained of its forces – three tank squadrons and one complete infantry company plus elements of a second – had secured Hill 195 without a fight and had begun to dig in. The defensive location they chose was a large rectangular field surrounded by a classic formidable Norman bocage tree-hedge. Sadly the high ground Worthington Force had secured was neither Hill 195 nor any other hill close to this objective. In reality, Worthington Force had unwittingly captured the Thirty Acres area around Point 111 and Point 122, located on the north-east fringes of the Hill 140 ridge feature. This latter ridge extended east-north-

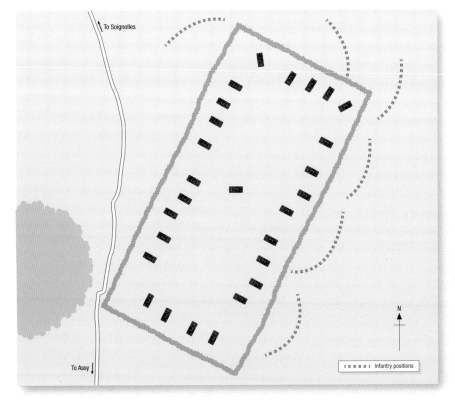

The lost and isolated Worthington Force formed a defensive position within a large hedge/tree-lined rectangular field in the Thirty Acres area of the Hill 140 ridge feature. The Sherman tanks took position inside the perimeter, while the infantry platoons dug in just outside of this perimeter.

east for 4,000m from Ouilly-le-Tesson until Rouvres; its southern slopes descended into the valley of Le Laison River. Incredibly, Thirty Acres was located 4,800m east of the main Caen–Falaise road, whereas Hill 195 was situated 1,700m west of this road. Worthington Force was racing towards its 'objective' not realising that Hill 195 was actually a staggering 6,600m away. The fact that no one on the Allied side knew that Worthington Force was horribly lost set in motion an unfortunate series of events that sealed its fate.

For back at 0600hrs, SS officers manning the 'Hitlerjugend' division's Laison Gorge OPs had spotted on the horizon the dense dust clouds kicked up by Worthington Force's vehicles as they approached Point 122. A startled Kurt Meyer ordered an immediate counter-attack against this shockingly deep Allied penetration of the German line. Reacting swiftly, by 0720hrs two groups of tanks had moved out from Quesnay Wood. They were to link up with Waldmüller's Panzergrenadiers from I Bataillon, SS-Panzergrenadier-Regiment 25 who had deployed across the Hill 140 area to form two improvised battle groups. The mission given to these task forces was to destroy Worthington Force before Allied reinforcements arrived on the vital high ground of Thirty Acres.

The first battle group of 18 tanks and two infantry companies from SS-Panzergrenadier-Regiment 25 headed east-north-east from La Grosse Gerbe towards the summit of Hill 140 to strike Worthington Force from the south-west. The second group of eight Tiger tanks moved south-west along the road to Les Maisons Neuves where around 0730hrs it linked up with a third company from I Bataillon, SS-Panzergrenadier-Regiment 25. This enemy battle group moved east-north-east along the road that skirted Hill 140's southern slopes until it reached Le Logis Château. Here, the force swung north-north-west through the open fields to approach the Canadian position from the south-east and east. By around 0800hrs, meanwhile, 12 Worthington Force Shermans had moved forward (south) 800m to assume defensive positions within Thirty Acres Wood. With excellent observation across the ridge's southern slopes, the Shermans' evident mission was to dominate the southern and eastern approaches to the main Worthington Force defensive position in the rectangular field.

Just as these Shermans arrived at Thirty Acres Wood, the Tigers engaged them from the south-east from a range of 1,000m; within 20 minutes accurate enemy tank fire had knocked out all 12 Shermans. By 0840hrs, Worthington Force had meanwhile informed 4th Canadian Armoured Brigade that it was under attack and requested that artillery fire support be brought down on the enemy, now located just 450m south-east of its position. Allied artillery responded swiftly with accurate concentrations – that landed on Hill 195's southern slopes, 6,600m west-south-west of Point 122. But when at 0907hrs, 4th Canadian Armoured Brigade contacted Worthington Force to gauge the accuracy of the fire support they were met with silence; the task force's wireless sets had presumably been destroyed by enemy fire.

View of Thirty Acres Wood, the outpost position for the Worthington Force defensive perimeter. Some 12 Sherman tanks moved forward to this position to dominate the southern approaches to Worthington's main force, but all 12 were knocked out within minutes by accurate German Tiger and Panther tank fire. (Author's collection)

During the next hour various elements from the two SS battle groups spread out, all but surrounding Worthington Force. Presumably sensing that the Allied force stood little chance of escape, the German tanks next pulled back. Subsequently, throughout the rest of the morning the Panzers poured long-range tank fire onto Worthington Force, supplemented with mortar and artillery fire, while the Shermans responded ferociously, depleting their limited stocks of ammunition. The German fire knocked out a dozen Shermans and inflicted heavy personnel casualties. Realising that his many wounded could not be treated in such conditions, Worthington ordered his few still-operational half-tracks to carry them to safety by courageously breaking out towards the north-west. Miraculously, the column successfully escaped through the gauntlet of enemy fire back to the Polish 1st Armoured Division's lines. Somehow news that Worthington Force personnel had reached Allied lines failed to make its way up the chain of command. Consequently, the missing Worthington Force remained lost both to itself and to the Allied command.

To make matters worse, Allied fighter bombers then attacked Worthington Force, understandably not expecting to find friendly forces in this location. After Worthington's mortar crews warned off the Typhoons with yellow identification smoke, the latter repeatedly returned to strafe the nearby German positions. Unfortunately, news of where this friendly force was located failed to reach II Canadian Corps via First Canadian Army from the 84th Group chain of command. Despite these clues Worthington Force remained lost to all on the Allied side.

Throughout the early afternoon long-range German tank fire continued to engulf Worthington Force's position. This fire exerted a steady toll on the Canadians until by around 1430hrs just eight of the 39 tanks that had reached Thirty Acres remained operational, and these had all but run out of ammunition. Worthington now ordered these eight tanks to mount a desperate breakout attempt, and somehow the tanks managed to evade the German fire as they raced north to reach the safety of the nearby Polish lines. The information thus garnered concerning the location of Worthington Force subsequently led to two, abortive, rescue bids being made to reach the beleaguered battle group.

Around 1830hrs the Germans mounted another determined infantry assault on the remnants of Worthington Force that was backed by intense tank fire. Every Canadian soldier still capable of firing a weapon, including the wounded and the tank crews whose vehicles had been wrecked, fought back desperately with small arms and grenades, and managed to drive off this latest assault, although in the process Worthington was fatally injured. Around 2030hrs, as dusk descended on the battlefield, repeated enemy assaults finally overran the Canadian position. In this final encounter, only two groups of seven Canadian soldiers, each led by a lieutenant, managed to fight their way out through the encircling forces to reach the nearby Polish positions. Worthington Force had effectively been annihilated.

Lieutenant-Colonel Donald Worthington, the commander of the ill-fated Worthington Force, died while organising his lost task force's desperate resistance to repeated SS Panzer onslaughts. He is buried at the Canadian Military Cemetery near Bretteville-sur-Laize. (Author's collection)

GERMAN COUNTER-ATTACK AGAINST THE DEFENSIVE PERIMETER OF WORTHINGTON FORCE, 9 AUGUST 1944 (PP. 80–81)

This scene shows a German counter-attack against the defensive perimeter of the beleaguered Worthington Force. Four Panther tanks **(1)** from the 12.SS-Panzer-Division 'Hitlerjugend', with Panzergrenadiers running alongside them **(2)**, are advancing, main guns blazing, towards the Canadian perimeter (comprising a classic Norman tree-hedge). The action was a desperate last stand by the lost and isolated Worthington Force in which the defenders were virtually annihilated.

Shown here are the rears of three Sherman tanks **(3)** deployed behind the perimeter tree-hedge. Two of the Shermans are burning from hits from the Panther's main 75mm gun. On the left rear of the Shermans can be seen their divisional insignia **(4)** (a brown maple leaf on green) and on the right the tactical sign '53' in white on red **(5)**.

Back at 0914hrs that morning Kitching had reacted with alarm to the news of the enemy counter-attacks against Worthington Force. Consequently at 1030hrs 4th Canadian Armoured Brigade ordered the Shermans of the Governor General's Foot Guards to form up at Gaumesnil with the single Algonquin company that had dropped away from Worthington Force during the night to create another improvised battle group. This task force was given the mission of advancing south-south-west to Hill 195 to rescue Worthington's surrounded troops. Incredibly, it took until 1430hrs for the battle group's various elements to assemble, despite exhortations to speed up the process. Finally, at 1430hrs this battle group advanced south, overcoming weak enemy resistance to reach the defile that ran south-south-west from Langannerie to Bretteville-le-Rabet by 1500hrs. Here, the Canadians encountered an enemy infantry company position bolstered by a Tiger tank and several anti-tank guns. The enemy blocking position held off the Canadian advance until dusk, when the Shermans withdrew north into a defensive laager for the night. This rescue attempt neither encountered any elements of Worthington Force nor ascertained that Worthington Force was not actually on Hill 195.

As this futile rescue bid towards Hill 195 unfolded, the Canadians also attempted other relief efforts that reflected their growing suspicion that Worthington Force was actually somewhere near Hill 140, not Hill 195. At 1330hrs, Canadian Grenadier Guard Shermans, which had just withdrawn from Halpenny Force's attacks on Bretteville-le-Rabet, advanced south-east from Cauvicourt towards Hill 140. By 1615hrs the Shermans had advanced 2,300m to cross the exposed fields located between Bretteville-le-Rabet and Estrées-la-Campagne. Here, however, the Shermans were caught by murderous enemy tank and anti-tank fire that knocked out 26 vehicles in 10 minutes; not surprisingly, the surviving tanks withdrew north back out of this killing zone. The failure of this rescue bid, therefore, ensured that Worthington's troops were left to face their terrible fate alone.

Despite its heroic resistance, and the abortive rescue bids described above, Worthington Force's last stand left the force decimated. At various times that day small groups had managed to exfiltrate back to Allied lines, but this amounted to around just 120 personnel. During Worthington Force's advance to, and defence of, the Thirty Acres position it suffered over 200 personnel casualties and lost no fewer than 44 AFVs. The fact that a bizarre combination of bad luck and Allied misunderstandings had contributed to the brutal demise of Worthington Force only compounded the poignancy of these losses. Yet what shone out to offset these, however, was the astonishing courage displayed by Worthington's troops in the face of appalling adversity.

Other Phase II operations

While the 4th Canadian Armoured Division endeavoured to rescue Worthington Force during 9 August, its main focus remained the execution of other operations designed to secure the starting points required for any subsequent drive towards the high ground north of Falaise. Throughout that morning Halpenny Force battled to overcome fierce enemy resistance in Bretteville-le-Rabet, which was finally cleared at 1405hrs. Next, at 1500hrs a squadron of South Alberta Shermans, together with 1st Argyll and Sutherlands infantry, advanced south from Bretteville-le-Rabet to assault Langannerie. Simultaneously, the infantry of the Lincoln and Welland Regiment, together with another South Alberta Sherman squadron, struck south-west to assault the villages of Vieille-Langannerie, Grainville-Langannerie and Grainville. After a series of bitter engagements the Canadian forces eventually secured all four villages.

Rather than allow the exhausted Argyll and Lincoln infantrymen to dig in for the night of 9/10 August, a still angry Simonds instead ordered them both to continue operations throughout the hours of darkness. He ordered the Lincoln and Wellands to advance 2,100m south-west from Grainville-Langannerie to seize the key terrain of Hill 180. Simonds simultaneously directed the 1st Argyll and Sutherlands to advance to capture Hill 195, which by then the Allies knew Worthington Force had not secured. Despite losing formational cohesion in the dark, the weary Lincoln and Wellands successfully marched south to reach the northern slopes of Hill 180, where they subsequently dug in.

Subsequently, at 2359hrs, the 1st Argyll and Sutherlands commenced an audacious surprise covert night march onto the north-east corner of Hill 195. During the next five hours they marched in silence, infiltrating through the enemy lines until they reached the fringes of Hill 195. They reached the objective without firing a round or sustaining a single casualty, and then feverishly dug defensive positions in the short time that remained before dawn arrived. By daybreak, moreover, some towed Canadian anti-tank guns reached the 1st Argyll and Sutherlands' positions and these provided the long-range anti-tank capability required to repel the predictable enemy armoured counter-strikes. With hindsight, the success of this night infiltration to Hill 195 – in contrast to Worthington Force's abject failure – reveals what impact a single piece of bad luck can have on mission accomplishment during the chaos that bedevils night-time operations.

In this poignant depiction of soldiers' dark battlefield humour, Corporal Jack Reay of No. 2 Provost Company, Canadian Provost Corps, paints a sign that reads: 'Old Soldiers Never Die – They Dig! And Fade Away Into a Slit Trench', on 13 August 1944. (Library and Archives Canada PA-132414)

By dawn on 10 August the Shermans of the Governor General's Foot Guards were already on their way to reinforce the 1st Argyll and Sutherlands on Hill 195, before pushing a further 2,300m south-east to secure Hill 206. But before they could arrive, the Panzergrenadiers of III Bataillon, SS-Panzergrenadier-Regiment 26, mounted a series of furious assaults on the 1st Argyll and Sutherlands' positions, supported by Goliath remote-controlled demolition vehicles and intense Nebelwerfer fire. The Foot Guards' Shermans managed to break through to the beleaguered 1st Argyll and Sutherlands and throughout the day the hard-pressed Canadian forces, backed by repeated artillery concentrations and tactical air strikes, repelled every enemy assault on the hill, inflicting grievous casualties in the process. By dusk, Hill 195 had been held, although the ferocity of the German response also made it clear that Simonds' aspiration that the Foot Guards press forward to Hill 206 was completely unrealistic.

At the same time as the 4th Canadian Armoured Division's operations unfolded during 9 August, the Polish 1st Armoured

The final result, 7–11 August 1944.

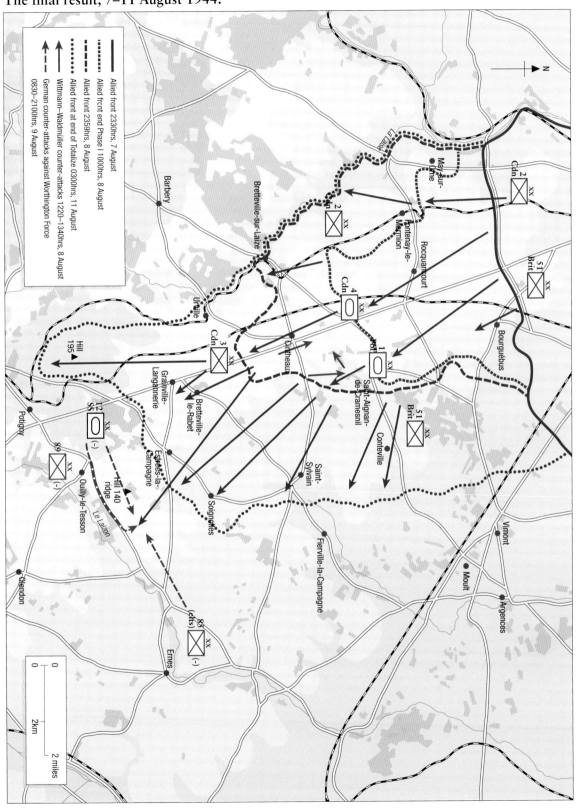

Allied front 2330hrs, 7 August
Allied front end Phase 1 1000hrs, 8 August
Allied front 2359hrs, 8 August
Allied front at end of Totalize 0300hrs, 11 August
Wittmann–Waldmüller counter-attacks 1220–1340hrs, 8 August
German counter-attacks against Worthington Force
0830–2100hrs, 9 August

Division recommenced its advance south across the sector located beyond the eastern environs of the main Caen–Falaise road. At 1220hrs the Polish spearhead units located on either side of Renémesnil commenced their assaults south onto the enemy positions located on either side of Saint-Sylvain, which were held by elements of Kampfgruppe Waldmüller. The mobile firepower in this part of the German front was provided by nine Jagdpanzer IV tank destroyers of 1.Kompanie, SS-Panzerjäger-Abteilung 12. In addition, the infantry element was provided by the escort companies of 12.SS-Panzer-Division 'Hitlerjugend' and I SS-Panzerkorps.

After four hours of bitter fighting in which 10 Polish tanks were knocked out, the determinedly pressed Polish attacks succeeded in securing all of Saint-Sylvain. Pushing further south, the continuing Polish attacks managed to outflank to the west the enemy positions around Soignolles. Despite this increasingly unfavourable battlefield situation, elements of the 'Hitlerjugend' escort company continued to mount a ferocious defence of the village of Soignolles through to the onset of darkness. Meanwhile, operating on an axis located a further 1,100m to the west, other Polish units pushed forward on a south-westerly bearing to close on the village of Estrées-la-Campagne. It was the sanctuary of the front held by these units around Estrées-la-Campagne that Worthington Force's remaining eight tanks, all out of ammunition, somehow managed to break through the encircling German forces to reach around 1450hrs.

Subsequently, between 1500 and 2000hrs, Polish armour and infantry attempted to press forward towards the Hill 140 hill feature where the beleaguered Worthington Force was still fighting for its life. However, these attempted advances across the open fields located south-west of Estrées-la-Campagne were stymied by a sustained hail of accurate German tank and mortar fire. By the first hints of approaching dusk around 2030hrs, the Polish forces located north-west of Hill 122 had begun to prepare defensive positions for the night. Just as they were doing so, two sections of exhausted and bedraggled Algonquin infantrymen reached the Polish lines with the gravely disturbing news that Worthington Force's heroic defensive last stand had finally been overwhelmed by the most recent enemy assaults.

The offensive ends

Despite the successful capture and holding of Hill 195 during 10 August, Simonds still remained frustrated at the degree of offensive momentum achieved during Totalize Phase II. Late that morning, therefore, he issued new orders for the mounting of a decisive assault that he hoped would restore the speed of his corps' advance. He instructed 3rd Canadian Infantry Division to mount a hastily improvised set-piece thrust south-east from Langannerie through Quesnay

A dispatch rider, identified as Lance-Corporal Bill Baggott, sleeps precariously balanced on his motorcycle somewhere within the Totalize battle zone on 13 August 1944. One must assume that only an exhausted individual could actually sleep in such an uncomfortable position. (Library and Archives Canada PA-161885)

Wood, across the Laison River near Ouilly-le-Tesson, to secure the north–south ridge located east of the main Caen–Falaise road between Tassily and Aubigny. Quesnay Wood provided a much-needed sanctuary for German armour from the devastating Allied tactical air strikes. With much of I SS-Panzerkorps' remaining Panzers concentrated within the wood, the position formed a powerful central bastion that dominated the main Caen–Falaise road and upon which the Germans could hinge their infantry defensive positions to either side. The 8th Canadian Infantry Brigade was slated to initiate the assault, with the Queen's Own Rifles of Canada

and the North Shore Regiment spearheading the assault. The Shermans of 2nd Canadian Armoured Brigade were to support the division during this attack. In addition, two complete Army Groups, Royal Artillery were to provide fire support for the renewed offensive, although the limited available planning time meant that the fire plan was inevitably a rather rushed affair.

The Queen's Own Rifles and North Shores both experienced delays forming up, and the fire-support planning could not be done in the limited time Simonds had set. As a result, the attack on Quesnay Wood could only be commenced at 2000hrs, when darkness would soon be approaching. This was hardly an auspicious manner in which to initiate a major set-piece assault. Despite the increasing darkness and the dearth of intelligence concerning the enemy, both Canadian infantry battalions nevertheless determinedly fought their way into the northern fringes of the wood. The enemy responded quickly, however, initiating a number of fierce counter-strikes mounted by platoons of SS-Panzergrenadiers backed by a troop of tanks. By 2200hrs, these enemy ripostes had managed to drive most of the Canadian forces north out of the woods. Some elements of the North Shores, however, repelled several local German ripostes throughout the night to maintain a small foothold in Quesnay Wood's northern fringes through to daylight. Simonds' attempt to restore momentum to Totalize had clearly failed and the viability of continuing the offensive now seemed questionable. By 0330hrs on 11 August the corps commander had bowed to the inevitable. He now reluctantly accepted the unfavourable battlefield realities that his forces faced, and thus cancelled the offensive, which had now obviously stalled irrevocably. After 76 hours of bitter conflict, Totalize was over.

The band of the 3rd Canadian Division headquarters, seated on the left, plays music outside Château Beauregard, as some of the division's officers visit the newly opened leave camp. (Library and Archives Canada PA-169345)

Conclusion

It would be fair to describe Totalize as a rather paradoxical operation of stark contrasts. The innovation evident in Phase I's audacious surprise night-time assault spearheaded by infiltrating mobile columns delivered an impressively swift and casualty-light break-in of the powerful German initial defensive position. The subsequent initiation of Phase II in the early afternoon of 8 August seemed to offer the Allies a fleeting opportunity to translate this tactical success into a decisive advance to Falaise, an achievement that might

have had considerable operational-level significance. However, the success of meagre German forces in stymieing the advance of Simonds' armour during the afternoon of the 8th meant that this opportunity slipped through his fingers.

Simonds' response to this setback was a desperate, risk-embracing attempt to restore forward momentum by mounting an impromptu repetition of the previous night's set-piece mobile column infiltration assault. This not only merely achieved modest success but also led to the most tragic aspect of Totalize – the decimation of the hopelessly lost and isolated Worthington Force. Subsequent Allied assaults during 9–10 August gained further ground but never restored much forward momentum to the flagging offensive. By the termination of Totalize early on 11 August, some 76 hours after its initiation, II Canadian Corps' forces had secured an impressive 16,200m advance across a 14,200m frontage. The offensive, however, had only secured but one fraction of the high ground north of Falaise that had been its stated objective. Thus the key lateral road that ran eastward through that town remained undominated by Allied artillery fire and thus remained available to the desperate German forces then flooding east to escape from the looming encirclement of what would become known as the 'Falaise pocket'.

Personnel from the Rear Headquarters of the 2nd Canadian Infantry Division cluster round a jeep to listen to the British Broadcasting Corporation news from London. This image was apparently taken at Laize-la-Ville, on 12 August 1944, just after Totalize had ended. (Library and Archives Canada PA-140193)

An Allied 6pdr anti-tank gun and an ambulance lorry marked by its red cross parked in a square within a bombed-out village near the Totalize start line on 11 August 1944. (Library and Archives Canada PA-132911)

The aftermath of Operation Totalize, 11–29 August 1944.

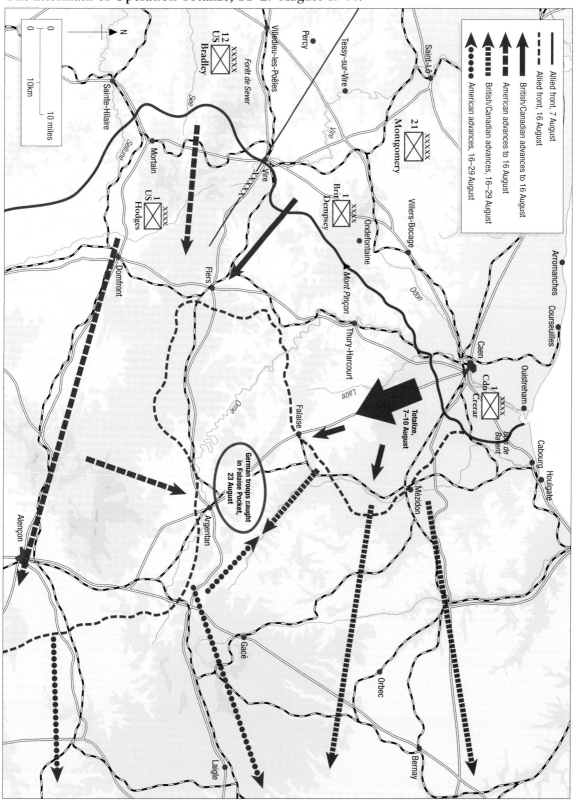

AFTERMATH

On the same day that Totalize ended – 11 August – General Montgomery issued a new directive (M518) for subsequent 21st Army Group operations. This directive ordered First Canadian Army to capture the town of Falaise and then Argentan, thus completing the encirclement of enemy forces in Normandy by linking up with the northward advancing American forces around Argentan. Directive M518 also revealed Montgomery's intent to enact, together with the Americans, a wider and deeper encirclement of German forces by pinning them against the Seine River. There thus existed confusion among Montgomery's forces as to which of these two intents represented the main effort. To fulfil Directive M518, First Canadian Army ordered Simonds to mount another major firepower-reliant set-piece offensive towards Falaise.

Initiated on 14 August, Operation Tractable was essentially a daytime repetition of Totalize Phase I. The new offensive, however, used smoke – instead of darkness – to conceal the attacking forces as they closed to contact with the enemy, in order to minimise casualties at the hands of long-range enemy fire. During 14–15 August the 3rd Canadian Infantry Division and the 4th Canadian Armoured Division made steady, if not rapid, progress south across the Laison Valley towards Falaise. On the 15th, however, Simonds responded to a proposal by Major-General Maczek by launching the Polish 1st Armoured Division eastward, almost perpendicular to the main southward thrust of II Canadian Corps. Maczek's mission was to seize a bridgehead over the Dives River at Jort, which his forces duly achieved by the following morning.

By then, with the situation becoming more fluid, Simonds had already issued a new corps directive that ordered his two armoured divisions to strike in parallel rapidly south-eastwards to reach the Trun–Vimoutiers road. By 18 August the 4th Canadian Armoured Division had successfully advanced along the valley of the Dives to seize Trun and Saint-Lambert-sur-Dives. Meanwhile, the Polish 1st Armoured Division had advanced on an axis north-eastward of the Canadian division to close on the vital ground of the Mont Ormel ridge. On the previous day Montgomery had issued a new directive that ordered Simonds' two armoured divisions rapidly to close the Falaise pocket by advancing to Chambois

Many soldiers on both sides of the battle during Operation Totalize made the ultimate sacrifice in the service of their respective regimes' cause. Here the graves of dozens of Polish soldiers who lost their lives in Normandy can be seen in the Polish Military Cemetery at Urville-Langannerie. (Author's collection)

to link up with the northward American advance. Elements of the Polish 1st Armoured Division successfully linked up with the Americans at Chambois on the 19th, thus sealing the pocket. Other substantial elements of the Polish division meanwhile had become isolated on the Mont Ormel ridge. Over the ensuing 48 hours these Polish forces defended the ridge with remarkable tenacity against repeated, desperate German attacks to break out of the pocket. Despite the dogged defence of the Mont Ormel–Chambois sector mounted by Simonds' two armoured divisions, some 40,000 German personnel nevertheless managed to exfiltrate themselves out of the encirclement. Left in their wake, however, the Allies captured at least 60,000 troops in the Falaise pocket, while hundreds of heavy weapons were either destroyed or captured. This disaster left the remnants of the German Army in Normandy barely cohesive and thus scarcely able to impede even marginally the now headlong Allied advance towards the German Reich's western borders.

Infantry soldiers of Les Fusiliers Mont-Royal employ a jeep and towed tractor to carry French civilians who are being evacuated from the battle zone in the Falaise area, on 17 August 1944. (Library and Archives Canada PA-140211)

Meanwhile, during 16–19 August the US V Corps had advanced eastward to establish a bridgehead over the Seine River at Mantes-Gassicourt. Simultaneously, the north-eastern flank of First Canadian Army – British I Corps – had also begun to drive east towards the lower Seine. The demoralised and increasingly de-motorised German remnants that had managed to extricate themselves from the disaster at Falaise now faced the prospect of being annihilated in a geographically larger encirclement against the Seine. However, in a stunning display of improvisation, between 21 and 28 August the German remnants somehow managed to withdraw back to the Seine and extricate most of their remaining forces across the river without incurring catastrophic casualties.

Although by 29 August the Allies had inflicted a devastating defeat in Normandy, in which Totalize played its own small part, the successful enemy withdrawal across the Seine at least meant that a combat-experienced

An entry in the visitor's book of the Polish Military Cemetery at Urville-Langannerie shows that the soldiers' sacrifice during Totalize has not been forgotten: 'It is fortunate that the Poles were here [in 1944]! If not, then France would not be here today'. (Author's collection

cadre still existed from which the Germans could rebuild their defences in the West. By the time the Germans were able to reconstitute a cohesive defence in late September, the Allied forces had liberated the whole of France, much of Belgium and a few areas of the Netherlands. The Westheer was now locked into a desperate attritional defence of the western frontiers of the Reich itself. The achievements of Totalize had formed one small step along this Allied journey to liberate much of western Europe and take the battle into the heartlands of the Nazi Reich.

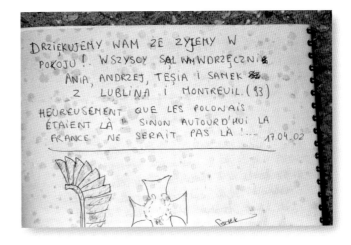

THE BATTLEFIELD TODAY

Unlike many of the Normandy battlefields closer to the coast, the area south of Caen has experienced much less post-war development, although substantial new housing estates have been built in May-sur-Orne and Fontenay-le-Marmion. In the agricultural areas between these villages, however, relatively little new housing has been built and large areas remain only slightly changed from their 1944 situation. Indeed in some places, such as Tilly-la-Campagne, farm buildings still bear the scars of the bitter fighting that raged in 1944. The battlespace over which Totalize was fought has also been obscured to a degree by the construction of several new roads and the installation of new telegraph wires and their associated pylons. Notwithstanding these caveats, the relative dearth of post-war development means that a modern visitor can usually still get a good sense of the terrain over which Totalize was fought.

The region features a number of promising locations from which to observe the actions fought during Totalize. One such spot is the memorial on Hill 67, located immediately west of the D562 road to the north of Saint-Martin-de-Fontenay. From here the visitor gets a good view of the road as it descends south towards Saint-André-sur-Orne, Saint-Martin-de-Fontenay and May-sur-Orne, providing a panorama of the operations on the offensive's western flank. From the area of the raised grass mound, a covered reservoir, located 90m east of the memorial, the visitor also gets an excellent view south-east across the open fields to the modern D89 lateral road which marks out II Canadian Corps' original start line. The distinctive Beauvoir Farm is clearly visible, marking the area from where the Canadian triple mobile column formation commenced its night advance. Similarly, if a visitor stands facing south-south-west on the southern end of the bridge that carries the now disused iron-ore railway line over the D89b road at Soliers, he/she will get a good view of the left British mobile column's initial advance.

View of the fields across the north-western approaches to the village of May-sur-Orne, over which Les Fusiliers Mont-Royal advanced during three separate assaults mounted on 8 August 1944. (Author's collection)

Another good vantage point is the western fringes of Hill 122, located adjacent to the eastern carriageway of the main N158 road (which follows the path of the 1944 Caen–Falaise road) north-west of Cramesnil. A visitor looking west from here will get an excellent view of the southward advance of the Royals' and Hamiltons' mobile columns from Rocquancourt (whose church steeple is a clear reference point). The visitor can trace their advance south along the tracks beyond the railway embankment down to the debus area. The visitor can also see in the forefront the fields of Longues Rayes across which the Royals assaulted onto Hill 122 in the first fully tracked APC-mounted Anglo-Canadian infantry assault of the war. From Hill 122's northern fringes, moreover, the visitor also gets a sense of the southward advance of the British mobile columns.

View from the German defensive positions on the key terrain of Hill 122, looking north along the axis of what then was the main Caen–Falaise road, now a dual carriageway. Across this terrain the Canadian and British forces advanced on the viewer's left- and right-hand sides of the road, respectively. (Author's collection)

Another promising location from which to view the transition from the offensive's first phase to its second is to be found in the Delle-de-la-Rocque orchards located south-west of Saint-Aignan-de-Cramesnil. Looking south-west towards the isolated red-roofed building adjacent to the N158 road, the visitor can observe the location where Michael Wittmann's Tiger tank was destroyed and the SS-Panzer ace killed. Walking 360m east-south-east the visitor can also enter the peculiar Le Petit Ravin U-shaped ravine to imagine the bitter tank battle fought there in the early afternoon of 8 August.

Moving south, a visitor can get a good sense of how German knowledge of the local terrain enabled them to select excellent locations for OPs and HQs. Meyer chose Château Le Mont Joly, located south of Saint-Quentin, as his division HQ. Some 200m west of this HQ the Germans established an OP on top of the *Tombeau de Marie Joly* shrine, perched on the eastern edge of the Laison Gorge which gave excellent views to the north; just 100m west across the gorge the Germans also established a second OP at the rocky outcrop of La Brèche au Diable. It was from these two OPs that SS personnel spotted the advance of Worthington Force at first light on 9 August, setting in action the sequence of events that led to the isolated Canadian battle group's destruction.

This latter tragedy is commemorated by a monument located along the D131 road south-east of Soignolles, which is easily spotted by the Canadian flags flying from its twin flag poles. The actual ground over which Worthington Force made its heroic last stand is located some 550m south of the monument – in the now open fields just to the north-north-east of the small wooded copse by Point 122. Some 900m south-south-east is a small wood, now dubbed Thirty Acres Wood, which was the Worthington Force outpost position. From here the visitor gets excellent views of the southern fringes of the Hill 140 feature as they descend into the wooded Laison river valley. There are, therefore, a number of locations from which the modern visitor can obtain excellent views of the ground over which the key actions of Totalize were fought.

View of the inscription on the *Worthington Force Monument*, which acknowledges the incredible courage demonstrated by the personnel of this isolated force as its defensive last-stand was overwhelmed by repeated SS armoured attacks. (Author's collection)

WORTHINGTON FORCE

On the 9 August 1944, in phase 2 of the Operation Totalize, Worthington Force, 28 th Armoured regiment (The British Columbia Regiment) and the Algonquin Regiment as part of the 4th Canadian Armoured Division was tasked with securing the high ground overlooking Falaise. On and around Hill 140, Worthington Force fought a desperate and stubborn engagement against a most determined enemy. Their courage and sacrifice remains unsurpassed in the annals of the Canadian Army.

LE GROUPEMENT WORTHINGTON

Le 9 Août 1944, en phase 2 de l'opération Totalize, les chars du colonel Worthington, 28e Régiment blindé canadien (Régiment de Colombie Britannique) et le régiment de l'Algonquin tous deux à la 4e division blindée canadienne avaient pour mission de capturer les crêtes dominant Falaise. Autour de la côte 140, le groupe Worthington s'illustra en un farouche combat contre un ennemi qui lui était supérieur. Ce combat désespéré au prix d'un courageux sacrifice demeure unique dans les annales de l'armée canadienne.

FURTHER READING

Primary sources
The UK National Archives, Kew, London
CAB106, Cabinet Office Papers
WO171, War Office: British War Diaries
WO179, War Office: Canadian War Diaries
The Tank Museum Archive, Bovington
RAC Regiment War Diaries
Libraries and Archives Canada, Ottawa
RG24, Canadian War Diaries
General H. D. G. Crerar Papers
Brigadier C. Mann Papers
Published primary sources
Borthwick, Alastair, *Battalion: A British Infantry Unit's Actions from El Alamein to the Elbe, 1942–1945*, Bâton Wicks: London, 1994
Ellis, Major L. F., *Victory in the West*, Vol. I (*History of the Second World War*, UK Military series), HMSO: London, 1962
Foster, Tony, *Meeting of Generals*, Methuen: Toronto, 1986
Kitching, Major-General George, *Mud and Green Fields: The Memoirs of Major General George Kitching*, Battleline: Langley, BC, 1986
Meyer, Kurt, *Grenadiers*, J. J. Fedorowicz: Winnipeg, 1994
Stacey, C. P., *Official History of the Canadian Army in the Second World War*, Vol. III: *The Victory Campaign*, The Queen's Printer: Ottawa, 1960
Tout, Ken, *The Bloody Battle for Tilly*, Alan Sutton: Stroud, 2000
——, *By Tank: D-Day to VE-Day*, Robert Hale: London, 2007
Secondary literature
Agte, Patrick, *Michael Wittmann and the Waffen-SS Tiger Commanders of the 'Leibstandarte' in WWII*, Stackpole: Mechanicsville, 2006
Copp, Terry, 'Reassessing Operation "Totalize"', *Legion*, September–October 1999
——, *Fields of Fire: The Canadians in Normandy*, University of Toronto Press: Toronto, 2003
Delaney, Douglas E., *Corps Commanders*, UBC Press: Vancouver, 2011
Dickson, Paul Douglas, *A Thoroughly Canadian General: A Biography of General H. D. G. Crerar*, University of Toronto Press: Toronto, 2007
Doherty, Richard, *None Bolder: The History of the 51st Highland Division in World War II*, Staplehurst: Stroud, 2006
English, John A., *The Canadian Army and the Normandy Campaign: A Study in the Failure of High Command*, Praeger: London, 1991
Graham, Dominick, *The Price of Command: The Biography of General Guy G. Simonds*, Stoddart: Toronto, 1993
Granatstein, Jack, *The Generals: The Canadian Army's Senior Commanders in the Second World War*, Stoddart: Toronto, 1993
Graves, Donald E., *S. Albertas: A Canadian Regiment at War*, Robin Brass: Toronto, 1998
Hart, Stephen A., *Montgomery and 'Colossal Cracks': The 21st Army Group in Northwest Europe 1944–45*, Praeger: London, 2001; Stackpole: Mechanicsville, 2007
——, 'Indoctrinated Nazi Teenaged Warriors: The Fanaticism of the 12th SS Panzer Division Hitlerjugend in Normandy, 1944', in M. Hughes and G. Johnson (eds), *Fanaticism and Conflict in the Modern Age*, Manchester University Press: Manchester, 2004, pp. 81–100
——, *Sherman Firefly versus Tiger: Normandy 1944* (Osprey Duel Series No. 2), Osprey Publishing: Oxford, 2007
Jarymowycz, R. J., 'Canadian Armour in Normandy: Operation "Totalize" and the Quest for Operational Maneuver', *Canadian Military History*, Vol. VII, No. 2, spring 1998, pp. 19–40
Jentz, Thomas L., *Panzertruppen: The Complete Guide to the Creation and Combat Employment of Germany's Tank Force, 1943–1945*, Schiffer Military History: Atglen, PA, 1996
Latawski, Paul, *The Falaise Pocket* (Battlezone Normandy), Sutton: Stroud, 2003
Meyer, Hubert, *Kriegsgeschichte der 12 SS-Panzerdivision 'Hitlerjugend'*, Munin Verlag: Osnabrück, 1982
Reynolds, Michael, *Steel Inferno: I-SS Panzer Corps in Normandy*, Spellmount: Staplehurst, 1997
Salmond, J. B., *The History of the 51st Highland Division*, Wm. Blackwood: Edinburgh, 1953
Taylor, Les, 'Wittman's Last Battle', *After the Battle* No. 48, 1985, pp. 46–52

INDEX